Is God Crying?

Nora Faye

TRILOGY CHRISTIAN PUBLISHERS

TUSTIN, CA

Trilogy Christian Publishers
A Wholly Owned Subsidary of Trinity Broadcasting Network
2442 Michelle Drive
Tustin, CA 92780

For information, address Trilogy Christian Publishing

Rights Department, 2442 Michelle Drive, Tustin, Ca 92780.

Trilogy Christian Publishing/ TBN and colophon are trademarks of Trinity Broadcasting Network.

For information about special discounts for bulk purchases, please contact Trilogy Christian Publishing.

Manufactured in the United States of America

Trilogy Disclaimer: The views and content expressed in this book are those of the author and may not necessarily reflect the views and doctrine of Trilogy Christian Publishing or the Trinity Broadcasting Network.

10 9 8 7 6 5 4 3 2 1

Library of Congress Cataloging-in-Publication Data is available.
ISBN 978-1-63769-346-9
ISBN 978-1-63769-347-6 (ebook)

Contents

You keep track of all my sorrows.
You have collected all my tears in your bottle.
You have recorded each one in your book.

Psalm 56:8 (NLT)

Sweet Karen ~
Thank you for your
loving support during
the writing of this
book.
          Revelation 21:4
"you are loved" Nola Faye

I wish to express my sincere heart of gratitude to my father, who spent a big portion of his life dedicated to the biblical and historical study of the end times. I applaud my mother who patiently listened to my father talk endlessly on the subject. They both went home to be with the Lord many years ago, and they are deeply missed.

Introduction

When my little granddaughter was about four years old, she attended my father's funeral with her parents. Following the funeral, we were gathered as a family, and it began to gently rain. As the rain drops fell, my little granddaughter suddenly looked up to the sky and asked, "Mommy, is God crying?" When my son shared this experience with me, my heart was warmed to think that my granddaughter had viewed God as a sensitive God and was crying with us. As I pondered this thought, it caused me to wonder if it were possible that God actually cries when we are hurt? For a big part of my life, I had imagined God looking down from heaven and watching me while I hurt, but I had never pictured Him as crying with me. I have since come to believe that God cries with us, especially when He sees the suffering of mankind on the earth. Jesus wept with Mary and Martha when their brother Lazarus died, even though Jesus knew that He would raise their brother from the grave.

Therefore, when Jesus saw her weeping, and the Jews who came with her weeping, He groaned in the spirit and was troubled. And He said, "Where have you laid him?" They said to Him, "Lord, come and see." Jesus wept. Then the Jews said, "See how He loved him!"

John 11:33-36 (NKJV)

Jesus was not just shedding a few little tears, He was groaning in His spirit, and His tears were convulsive tears. This tells me how deep His love is for all of us, my friends. I am convinced that Jesus was crying tears over the death of Lazarus, but Jesus was also crying for the emotional pain and grief that Mary, Martha, and the Jews were experiencing. Jesus was in their pain and experiencing the grief with them. Jesus already knew in advance that He was getting ready to raise Lazarus back to life. In Hebrews 5:7 (NIV), it says, "During the days of Jesus' life on earth, he offered up prayers and petitions with fervent cries and tears to the one who could save him from death, and he was heard because of his reverent submission." In this passage, we see Jesus weeping with fervent cries and with tears.

In the Gospel of Mark 7:34-35 (NKJV), we read that some people brought a man to Jesus for him to be healed, "Then, looking up to heaven, He sighed, and said to him, 'Ephphatha,' that is, 'Be opened.' Immediately his ears were opened, and the impediment of his tongue was loosed, and he spoke plainly." This man was deaf and could not talk, and the people begged Jesus to heal the man. After Jesus took the man away from the crowd, He touched his tongue, and He touched his ears. Jesus then looked up to heavens, and He sighed deeply. Why did Jesus sigh deeply before He healed the man? Perhaps Jesus was thinking about the perfect and beautiful creation that God had made, which was ruined by the fall in the Garden of Eden. When He looked at this man, who had been hurt with the inability to hear or speak, it must have made the heart of Jesus cry. At that moment, God expressed His love and tears through a deep sigh. Is it possible that God cried in the Garden of Eden when He saw that His beautiful world was marred by one dreadful choice that man had made? Did God cry because His heart was breaking over the evil that had now made its way into the beautiful world that He had created? It makes me wonder if God is crying over His creation now as the biblical prophetic messages of the end times are unfolding? Does God weep for His people and yearn for them to stay alert as the labor pains are approaching?

I often have memories of when I was growing up and watching my father sit for hours at a time reading his Bible, from cover to cover. My father would endlessly and passionately talk about the end times with a fervent urgency in his voice. Occasionally, I would overhear him tell my mother that it was like a big giant puzzle, and the Holy Spirit was putting the pieces together for him. Many times my father would express his deep concern that many people may be caught off guard and be deceived in the latter days. As a young girl, I did not understand why these end-time events would cause my father to cry. As I study Bible prophecies, my understanding of why my father wept has become very clear to me. Just as my biological father wept, our heavenly Father weeps with us as we navigate all that is to come to pass before the return of Jesus. In the beginning, God created a beautiful world, and it was never in God's plan for the world to be so very broken.

My father's passion and urgency for people to know the truth prompted him to speak into a small cassette tape recorder all that he understood about the end times. Eventually, the tape recording transitioned into a small pamphlet booklet. The contents of the booklet were never edited, published, or distributed before he died in 1994. As I am writing this, my father's passion lives on inside of me.

A few years ago, I was prompted to process the message that my father was trying to share all of those years growing up. As I began to unwrap the truths in the writings of my father, I was awakened to the fact that this message concerning the end times was of extreme importance! As I began to edit, research, and cross-reference my father's writings, I began to see there was more information about the end times that I needed to explore. As the Holy Spirit guided me, that little booklet grew into eleven chapters about the vital events that will take place as the world approaches the latter days. This book is a combination of my father's writings and myself, collectively. The study of the end times can seem frightening to think that horrific times are eventually coming. On the other hand, it can be a comforting time for those who put their hope in God, knowing there is an eternal home where there will be no more sorrow, crying, or grief. As we look at the book of Genesis, the very first book in the Bible, we see where sin entered the world and brought about brokenness, violence, and death. When we look at the very last book in the Bible, the book of Revelation, we see a glorious ending! We can look forward to an end to this broken world and the beginning of an eternal place of peace to dwell in. Interpreting the end-time message can be complicated, and it lends itself to different views and theories. My father's view may seem totally different than others, and there is great respect for other people's perspectives. God did not want His church to be divided over this subject, and for that reason, I have kept an open mind and an open heart to the views of others.

CHAPTER 1

God's Recognition of World Empires

As I am writing this, I am in the middle of a "stay at home" order issued by the President of the United States. The entire world is experiencing a pandemic known as coronavirus, which has taken thousands of lives, sent our world economy into a downward tailspin, and shattered the emotions of people around the globe. It is a horrific tragedy like the world has never known before, and many people are questioning if this might be a sign for the end of time. Throughout the ages, especially in times of wars, plagues, and unusual weather patterns, questions do arise, such as: Are we going to heaven before the Antichrist is revealed? Will Christians go through the great tribulation? Is the great tribulation the same as the wrath of God? Is the Battle of Armageddon the same as the great tribulation? Who is the Antichrist and the false prophet? What is the abomination of desolation?

My hope is that questions like these will be answered in these writings. To understand the signs of the times, it is important to look into the pages of the Bible that point us in that direction. Through God's compassion for humanity, He issued compelling warnings about the end-time events. Just as God warned Noah about the coming flood and Jonah about the coming destruction of Nineveh, God also has warned us through the pages of the Bible. Out of His mercy and compassion, God used prophets and many other biblical characters to provide vital information about these end-time events. As we look forward to the return of our Lord Jesus Christ, it is important to examine and study all the events leading up to the Rapture of the church and the events following the Rapture. We will begin to navigate our way through the Bible to explore the signs, symbols, dreams, visions, and prophetic words that give us a picture of what is to come and how to be prepared.

God chose the prophets and other biblical characters to reveal to us the events surrounding the end times. One of those prophets was Daniel, whom God gave dreams and night visions. As we increase our knowledge about these things, those who know and are wise will instruct many.

His armed forces will rise up to desecrate the temple fortress and will abolish the daily sacrifice. Then they will set up the abomination that causes desolation. With flattery he will corrupt those who have violated the covenant, but the people who know their God will firmly resist him. Those who are wise will instruct many, though for a time they will fall by the sword or be burned or captured or plundered.

Daniel 11:31-33 (NIV)

I believe there is a time coming that people, including Christians, will have many questions about what is happening to the entire world, and as this passage indicates, those who understand will *instruct* many. In Matthew 21:1-36 (NIV), Jesus gave us a clear understanding of the signs of the time, and in verse 28, Jesus said, "When these things begin to take place, stand up and lift up your heads because your redemption is drawing near." As we process these events, it is not a time to be downcast, it is a time to stand up and look up for the coming of Christ is drawing near.

The events that surround the end times can be difficult to comprehend without knowing the history behind them. The Bible is overflowing with history from the beginning to the very end of God's Word. As we begin to look at the history of world empires, kings, nations, and prophecy, we will see how they all fit together leading up to the end of this age.

God recognizes world empires in the Bible, as they play a very significant role in the events leading up to the end of times. God begins to unfold the message they carry, even for us today, in the second chapter of Daniel. King Nebuchadnezzar was the reigning King over Babylon, and the king had a disturbing dream that troubled his mind, which left him sleepless. The king summoned all the wise men, magicians, and astrologers, and he ordered them to interpret the dream for him. The astrologers requested that the king tell them the dream, so they could interpret it. The King refused to tell them the dream and instead ordered them to tell him the dream and demanded them to interpret it. In Daniel 2:10 (NKJV), the Chaldeans answered the king: "The Chaldeans answered the king, and said, here is not a man on earth who can tell the king's matter; therefore no king, lord, or ruler has ever asked such things of any magician, astrologer, or Chaldean."

This made the king so furious that he ordered the execution of all the wise men of Babylon. The commander in chief Arioch had gone out to find Daniel so that Daniel and his friends could be put to death. Daniel had been brought from Judah to Babylon into captivity when King Nebuchadnezzar had overthrown Judah. Daniel was highly educated in all kinds of literature, and he was fully devoted to God. King Nebuchadnezzar had chosen Daniel and his friends to serve in the king's palace because they were full of wisdom and understanding. Daniel was also extremely gifted in understanding visions and dreams of all kinds. When Arioch went to put the wise men to death, Daniel spoke to him with wisdom and tact.

During the night, the mystery dream was revealed to Daniel by God. Daniel was able to approach King Nebuchadnezzar and not only tell him the dream, but he also was able to tell the king the meaning of the dream. God Almighty revealed everything about the king's dream to Daniel in a night vision.

Daniel told the king:

> You, O King, were watching; and behold, a great image! This great image, whose splendor was excellent, stood before you; and its form was awesome. This image's head was of fine gold, its chest and arms of silver, its belly and thighs of bronze, its legs of iron, its feet partly of iron, and partly of clay. You watched while a stone was cut out without hands, which struck the image on its feet of iron and clay, and broke them in pieces. Then the iron, the clay, the bronze, the silver, and the gold were crushed together, and became like chaff from the summer threshing floors; the wind carried them away so that no trace

was found. And the stone that struck the image became a great mountain and filled the whole earth.

Daniel 2:31-35 (NKJV)

The dream was prophetic in nature with symbols that represented world empires. God chose Daniel to be a prophetic voice for King Nebuchadnezzar as to which world empires would follow the King's rule over Babylon. Daniel then began to interpret Nebuchadnezzar's dream. Daniel told the king that God had given the king all dominion, power, and might over every living thing on earth and that he, Nebuchadnezzar, indeed was the head of gold.

The first symbol of gold represents the Babylonian World Empire that King Nebuchadnezzar himself ruled over. The next symbol was the chest and arms of silver and represents the Medio-Persian World Empire, which followed the Babylonian World Empire. The belly and thighs of bronze represent the Greek World Empire. The legs of iron represent the Roman World Empire.

As we can see, there are four world empires represented in the statue before it brings us down to the toes and feet.

> And as the toes of the feet were partly of clay,
> so the kingdom shall be partly fragile. As you
> saw iron mixed with ceramic clay, they will
> mingle with the seed of men; but they will not
> adhere to one another, just as iron does not
> mix with clay.
>
> Daniel 2:42-43 (NIV)

The toes and the feet represent another world empire that does not mix or adhere to the seed of men. The symbol of the mixture of iron and clay was quite unlike the other metals that Daniel saw in the dazzling statue. These two symbolic images have great significance in the end times. Please make a mental note of: "They will mingle with the seed of men, but they will not adhere to one another." This passage has a powerful impact on our understanding of the end times. We will revisit this portion of scripture as we unwrap these mysteries nestled within God's Word.

God chose to start with this great statue image in Nebuchadnezzar's dream to take us straight through to the rule of the Antichrist, the great tribulation, the Rapture, the wrath of God, the second coming of Christ, the battle of Armageddon, the thousand years of peace with Christ, and our eternal home in heaven. God wants us to understand all of the signs of the times that are going to take place and to understand what is coming upon this world. He never intended for the children of God to be in the dark, nor to be deceived concerning the last days.

In Mark 13:33 (NIV), Jesus had just explained the end times to His disciples, and then He warned them: "Be on guard! Be alert! You do not know when that time will come." In verse 37, Jesus said, "What I say to you, I say to everyone, Watch!" As we can see, Jesus let us know that we do not know when that time will come. However, Jesus was concerned that we could be easily deceived, and He did not want us to be found sleeping in the end times. We will begin to unpack the dreams and the visions in the book of Daniel to understand how they partner with John's visions and another prophetic book of Revelation in the Word of God.

CHAPTER 2

Daniel's Night Vision of a Fifth World Empire

Let's take a look at another dream that took place in the seventh chapter of Daniel, but this time it was Daniel's own dream and night vision. In Daniel 7:1-8, Daniel saw the four winds of heaven churning up the sea, and four great beasts, each different from the others, came up out of the sea. The first beast that he saw was a lion with the wings of an eagle. Daniel watched until its wings were plucked off, and it was lifted up from the earth. The eagle was made to stand on two feet like a man, and a man's heart was given unto it. The second beast was a bear with three ribs in its teeth. The third beast looked like a leopard with four wings on its back, like those of a bird. This beast had four heads, and it was given authority to rule. The fourth beast was a powerful creature that looked terrifying and fierce-looking.

It had large iron teeth, and it crushed and devoured its victims and trampled underfoot whatever was left. The fourth beast was different than the other beasts, and it had ten horns.

There are those who believe that chapter seven of Daniel is a repetition of chapter two, and the four beasts are the same as the symbols in the great dazzling statue. I disagree with that idea. However, I do agree with the idea that it is a continuation of chapter two. In my conclusion, there is no evidence to indicate that the two dreams have exactly the same meaning.

There are symbols in Nebuchadnezzar's dream that points to four world empires. I want to bring attention to the fact that there is a world empire missing in Nebuchadnezzar's dream but shows up in Daniel's night vision in chapter seven. I will try to give evidence of a fifth-world empire that does not show in the great dazzling statue image.

God chose to tell His message in this way to put a special emphasis on world empire number five because we are currently living in world empire number five today. The significance that God put on the world empire number five has been skimmed over, minimized, and neglected within the teaching realm for decades. Based on God's Word of truth, it is obvious to me that we are currently living in empire number five, and the next world empire will be number six and under the rule of the Antichrist.

World War II was the beginning of world empire number five, and the events of World War II brought about changes in the geographical maps of the world. It created a great three-way division of the nations of the world, as we know it today, namely the Free World, the Communist World, and the Third World. When you combine these three divisions together into one component, you truly have a one-world empire.

> Daniel said, "In my vision at night I looked, and there before me were the four winds of heaven churning up the great sea. Four great beasts, each different from the others, came up out of the sea. The first was like a lion, and it had the wings of an eagle. I watched until its wings were torn off and it was lifted up the ground so that it stood on two feet like a human being, and the mind of a human was given to it."
>
> Daniel 7:2-3 (NIV)

When God gave Daniel a night vision of four beasts coming up out of the sea, each different from the other, it was a vital message that God wanted His people to understand, especially as we move closer to the end times.

As I attempt to reveal their significance in our present time, let's take a look at what these symbols represent. The first great beast that Daniel saw in verse four was a lion with eagle's wings. God had not yet revealed a full-blown eagle to Daniel, just the eagle's wings on the back of the lion. Daniel observed until the wings were plucked out, and it was made to stand upon its feet as a man. It was lifted up from the earth, and a human heart was given unto it.

In my father's interpretation, and through the Holy Spirit's guidance, he believed the lion is a symbol of the old British Empire. He believed the eagle is a symbol of the United States of America. Over 200 years ago, there was no United States of America, but there was a British Empire. The sun never set on the possessions of the British Empire, and they were scattered all over the world. They had the greatest Navy fleet upon the planet, and they ruled the seas. Britain ruled over a big part of the world at that point in time, and there were thirteen colonies on the seaboard of what we call the USA today. The colonies were formed by people that were oppressed in other parts of the world for their religious beliefs and the way they worshipped God. Many of these oppressed people left their homelands and made their way to the New World, as it was called at that time. They were referred to as the Puritans, the Pilgrims, and other groups of people that put the thirteen

colonies in place, even though they were still possession of Great Britain. The vision that Daniel saw puts
the British Empire and America in the Bible and plays a
big part in the end times.

On October 19, 1781, British General Charles Corn-
wallis surrendered his Military Army to George Wash-
ington, the first President of the United States of
America and also the Commander-in-Chief of the Revolutionary War. The forces of the thirteen colonies, as
small as they were, fought against Great Britain and
won the battle for independence! They formed the
Constitution with its laws and rules as guidelines to
live by, and that was the beginning of the United States
of America. It was very small in the beginning, but as
God's hand was on the USA, it began to flourish, pros-
per, and grow rapidly.

Daniel observed that the wings were plucked out
of the lion, and it was lifted up from the earth, and a
man's heart was given unto it. We can certainly understand how eagles can be lifted up by their large wing-
span. The two eagle's wings that were plucked from
the lion were symbolic of the separation of the United
States of America and Great Britain. Great Britain became a shadow of what they were at that point in time,
and much of their empire had weakened. On the other
hand, the United States of America continued to grow
in power, resources, and influence. America has often

been referred to as a superpower nation. I would like to enlarge a little here on some of the attributes of America and the generous giving heart that it has always had and still does today. Consider for a moment how many other countries and nations of the world have been blessed by America's big heart.

America has always been ready to respond to the crisis of our neighbors (even their enemies) around the world in times of drought, floods, hurricanes, or other catastrophic events. America has fed, clothed, housed, and provided medical assistance to multitudes of people all around the globe and has done so with a generous heart.

There is another point that I want to make about the generosity of the United States of America. There are nations and countries around the globe that America spends millions of dollars on every year. Their generosity is a compassionate effort to get them on their feet to where they can feed themselves, lift up their heads with a higher standard of living, and value themselves among other nations. The big heart that Daniel saw in his vision represents the United States of America. Hold onto these thoughts as we look at the significance this will play in the end times.

In verse 5, Daniel saw a second beast which looked like a bear which was raised up on one of its sides and had three ribs in its mouth between its teeth: "And there before me was a second beast, which looked like a bear. It was raised up on one of its sides, and it had three ribs in its mouth between its teeth. It was told, 'Get up and eat your fill of flesh!'" This bear is a symbol of what is called Russia and could include other Communist countries such as Red China, North Korea, and others.

In verse 6, Daniel saw the third beast: "After that, I looked, and there before me was another beast, one that looked like a leopard. And on its back, it had four wings like those of a bird. This beast had four heads, and it was given authority to rule." The leopard that Daniel saw is a symbol of what is referred to as the Third World.

We can clearly see that these three beasts represent a three-way division of the nations of the world. Before World War II, this three-way division of world nations did not exist. The very first hint of this was brought about by Winston Churchill, who was the Prime Minister of England and Commander in Chief of the armed forces for the British Empire during World War II. Winston Churchill was invited to the little town of Fulton, Missouri, in March of 1946 to dedicate the Westminster College after a very popular colleague somewhere in the British Isles, and he accepted the invitation. Because of Churchill's stature and high visibility, the social media flocked to this special dedication event to capture every word of Winston Churchill. At that ceremony,

Winston Churchill coined this phrase, "A great Iron Curtain has been stretched from Stettin in the Baltic, to Trieste in the Adriatic." It took a little time for them to understand what Churchill's comment was referring to. World War II was over, and Russia had taken over a large part of Eastern Europe. Russia did not give up any of the Eastern European territories. Mr. Churchill coined that phrase because he recognized that there was a different world altogether on the other side of the Iron Curtain. On one side of the curtain was the Communist World, and on the other side of the curtain was the Free World. The world eventually accepted Churchill's concept and began to refer to that territory as the "Communist World" for simplification of identification purposes. The Free World countries were foundationally Christian, and the Judo-Christian principles were accepted as a way of life, while on the other side of the iron curtain, it was just the reverse.

At that time in history, the Russian government primarily resisted the idea of the religious freedom to worship God. However, in 1985 religious freedom was allowed by the government, and gospel went throughout Russia. Thousands of people were converted, and churches were established all over Russia. There is great affection for God in Russia today, and the people overflow with a deep love for their faith. The symbols in Daniel's vision of the eagle and the bear clearly represent these two world empires. The eagle represents America, and the bear represents Russia. Let's take a closer look at the leopard that Daniel saw in his vision.

In nineteen fifty-two, a French scientist coined the phrase "Third World" in reference to such countries as Africa, the Middle East, Latin America, and Asia. The article brought to attention the fact that there was a big part of the world that did not identify as the Communist World, nor did it line up with the Free World. There were a lot of nations that existed without identification, so they decided to refer to those nations as the "Third World." These nations are considered developing nations. I believe the leopard that Daniel saw in his vision was a symbol that stood for the Third World. For all these many years, those three worlds—the Free World, the Communist World, and the Third World— make up the entire world population. Currently, there is no human government outside of the Free World, the Communist World, and the Third World. Collectively, these three World Empires make up world empire number five.

Daniel describes three beasts that were in sequence: the lion, the bear, and the leopard, and in verses 7-8, Daniel describes a fourth beast that was terrifying, frightening, and very powerful.

After that, in my vision at night I looked, and there before me was a fourth beast-terrifying and frightening and very powerful. It had large iron teeth; it crushed and devoured its victims and trampled underfoot whatever was left. It was different from all the former beasts, and it had ten horns. While I was thinking about the horns, there before me was another horn, a little one, which came up among them; and three of the first horns were uprooted before it. This horn had the eyes like the eyes of a human being and a mouth that spoke boastfully.

Daniel 7:7-8 (NIV)

The ten horns are symbols of ten kingdoms that will join the little horn, which is a symbol of the Antichrist. The little horn is empire number six, and he will uproot and conquer the three world empires, which are collectively the Free World, the Communist World, and the Third World. He will set up a one-world order, and there will be no other government outside of world empire number six at that time in history.

In Nebuchadnezzar's dream, the first four world empires, the Babylonian Empire, the Medio-Persian Empire, the Greek Empire, and the Roman Empire followed each other, and each empire was more powerful than the one before them. In Daniel's dream, which reveals world empire number six, there is no time gap between world empire number five, which we are currently living in at the present time, and the sixth world empire. Once we establish the biblical fact that these symbols represent five world empires, the Babylonian, Medio-Persia, Greek, Roman, and the three collective empires, which make up world empire number five, we will see how the beast that Daniel saw is empire number six.

The Bible teaches six world empires under the devil's dominion, but when Christ and His church conquer the world at the Battle of Armageddon, world empire number seven will come into existence. The complete number of the devil is six, but God's complete number is seven, and His kingdom will last forever! When God sets up His kingdom, it will not pass to other people or other kingdoms because God's people are going to live forever and have immortal bodies that will never die. The kingdom of God is being built by the people who give their hearts and lives to the Lord Jesus Christ. Only those who are born of the spirit of God will make up kingdom number seven. This kingdom is an eternal kingdom, and those living in it will live eternally.

There was a man in the Bible named Nicodemus who asked about this eternal kingdom. Nicodemus was a ruler of the Jews and had seen the signs and miracles that Jesus had performed, and he knew that Jesus was a teacher sent from God. Even though Nicodemus was considered a religious Pharisee, he had questions for Jesus about how a person could get to heaven. When Jesus told Nicodemus that he must be born again, Nicodemus asked Jesus a reasonable question, "How can a man enter back into his mother's womb and be born?" Jesus replied, "Unless one is born of water and the Spirit, he cannot enter the kingdom of heaven." Jesus was very clear that we are born into this world through the flesh, but there is a second birth that is of the Spirit. Jesus promises eternal life to those who believe in Him. In John 6:47 (NKJV), Jesus said, "Most assuredly, I say to you, he who believes in me has everlasting life." The kingdom of God dwells within us the moment we accept Jesus as the only Lord and Savior. The kingdom of God is built on everlasting love, peace, and joy. These are the words of Jesus in John 8:12 (NKJV), "I am the light of the world. Whoever follows me will never walk in darkness, but will have the light of life." There is no need to fear the end times when we follow Jesus because He is light, and in Him there is no darkness at all. As we approach the end of this age, the world will become darker because of the rebellion against God. That is why the promises in these passages give us hope.

As we examine another vision that Daniel had, we will see how historical events line up with the prophetic end-time message. Just as God cries over the condition of the world and its rebellion, sin, hurt, rage, lawlessness, and brokenness, our hearts should be stirred to tears. Just like Nehemiah, who wept and mourned for days over the broken-down walls of Jerusalem and the condition of God's people, we can be moved to cry with God over this broken-down world.

Several years ago, I had a surgical procedure on my legs, and the doctor wrapped my legs in bandages before I was released to go home. The next day my daughter-in-law and my young granddaughter stopped by to check on my recovery. My daughter-in-law and her daughter sat across the room from me as we chatted. At one point, I noticed that my granddaughter began to tear up as she fixed her eyes on me. All of a sudden, my granddaughter jumped to her feet and quickly ran toward me. She threw herself on me and began sobbing. In my attempts to comfort her, I realized that my granddaughter's empathy toward me could not be contained. Just as my granddaughter's tears of compassion flowed out of a tender heart, God's tears cannot be contained. God's compassion flows out of His tender mercies toward us as He runs toward us.

CHAPTER 3

Daniel's Vision of the Ram and the Goal

Daniel had a second vision:

I looked up, and there before me was a ram with two horns, standing beside the canal, and the horns were long. One of the horns was longer than the other but grew up later. I watched the ram as it charged toward the west and the north and the south. No animal could stand against it, and none could rescue from its power. It did as it pleased and became great. I was thinking about this, suddenly a goat with a prominent horn between its eyes came from the west crossing the whole earth without touching the ground. It came toward the two horned ram I had seen standing beside the canal and charged at it with great rage. I saw it attack the ram furiously, striking the ram and shattering its two horns. The goat became very great, but at the height of its power the large horn was broken off, and in its place four prominent horns grew up toward the four winds of heaven.

Daniel 8:3-8 (NIV)

The vision that Daniel experienced is extremely significant in history and ties into the future events of the end times. Daniel saw a ram with two horns, and the horns were long. One horn was longer than the other, and it grew up last. The ram charged toward the west and the north and south. No one could stand against its power, and it did as it pleased. Daniel also saw a goat with a prominent horn between its eyes, and it attacked the ram furiously and trampled the ram. The goat symbolized the last king of the Grecian Empire, who was Alexander the Great. The ram represents the kingdoms that Alexander conquered, countries such as Persia, Egypt, Phoenicia, Judea, Gaza, and Mesopotamia. Some of the modern-day countries would fall under the regions of Turkey, Iraq, Iran, Syria, and other Middle East countries. He conquered everything in his sight, and then he wept when there were no more worlds for him to conquer. Alexander the Great died an untimely

23

death at the age of thirty-three, and the entire Grecian empire was divided up and given over to four Military Generals. In Daniel 8:8, it states that the goat became very great, but at the peak of its power, the horn was broken off, and in its place came four prominent horns. The four prominent horns were four Military Generals that took Alexander's position, and they created a four-way division of the Grecian Empire.

> Out of one of them came another horn, which started small but grew in power to the south and to the east and toward the Beautiful Land. It grew until it reached the heavens, and it threw some of the starry hosts down to earth and trampled on them. It set itself up to be as great as the commander of the army of the Lord; it took away the daily sacrifice from the Lord, and his sanctuary was thrown down. Because of the rebellion, the Lord's people and the daily sacrifice were given over to it. It prospered in everything it did, and truth was thrown to the ground.
>
> Daniel 8:9-12 (NIV)

antichrist

This small horn that takes away the daily sacrifice represents the one who will rise to global power and is referred to as the first beast or the Antichrist. It goes on to say:

> Then I heard a holy one speaking, and another holy one said to him, "How long will it take for the vision to be fulfilled—the vision concerning the daily sacrifice, the rebellion that causes desolation, the surrender of the sanctuary and the trampling underfoot of the Lord's people?"
>
> Daniel 8:13 (NIV)

Let's look at Daniel 11:2 (NKJV), where it says there are three kings yet in Persia, and the fourth shall be far richer than all. Then it goes on to tell what will transpire after that point in time. These three Kings in Persia are symbolic of the Free World, the Communist World, and the Third World. The fourth king represents the Antichrist, and it is the same man that is referred to as the beast in chapter thirteen of the book of Revelation. When he has gained power by his wealth, he will stir up everyone against the kingdom of Greece.

Unless we understand the meaning of the king of the South and the king of the North, it will be difficult to understand the history and formation of the world empires that we are currently living under at the present time. Let's take a look at what transpired during

World War II and how the eleventh chapter of the book of Daniel forms the foundation for the end of time.

I am going to present several high points that my father wrote without going into all the details of chapter eleven. He believed that in no uncertain terms, the Holocaust by Hitler, the London Blitz, the bombing of Pearl Harbor, and the rise of the Antichrist are represented in the eleventh chapter of Daniel. It also describes Hitler in his attempt to blow London off the map with serial raids. This is known as the London Blitz, which became one of the darkest hours of the British Empire. Hitler had already conquered France and was planning to fly over the English Channel before the USA got involved. Hitler made a move toward Russia and was moving close to Leningrad but got stopped by fierce weather. The German troops began to retreat and head back to Germany, which brought World War II to a head. History tells us that Hitler had a big bunker fort built in the middle of Berlin that was fifty feet underground, which had about sixty to seventy feet of reinforced concrete over the top of it. This bunker was to guarantee his safety during the war and to enable Hitler the privacy to continue his daily strategy meetings with his Military Generals.

When the Russian forces began to invade Germany from the east and were advancing closer to Berlin, Hitler retreated to the fort, where he later committed suicide. His aids then threw gasoline on Hitler and burned his remains until he could never be identified. In Daniel 11:19 (NKJV), which speaks directly about Adolf Hitler, it says, "Then he shall turn his face toward the fortress of his own land; but he shall stumble and fall, and not be found." Hitler could not be found when his fortress was invaded.

It goes on to say in verse 20: "There shall arise in his place one who imposes taxes on the glorious kingdom; but within a few days he shall be destroyed, but not in anger or in battle." As we read on through Daniel 11:21, it describes a vile person who rises to power peaceably and then seizes the kingdom by intrigue! "And in his place shall arise a vile person, to whom they will not give the honor of royalty; but he shall come in peaceably, and seize the kingdom." His successor will be a vile person who has not been given the honor of the royalty.

I cannot imagine what was going through Daniel's thoughts as these symbols of beasts, horns, kings, and daily sacrifices were revealed to him through a vision. God trusted this godly man with the events of the end times. It's hard to imagine how overwhelmed Daniel was as he saw these symbols and did not understand their meaning. Daniel inquired of the one standing there and asked him the meaning. The one standing there began to explain to Daniel what the vision meant. The vile man that is mentioned in this passage is the same one that John saw in his vision while on the island of Patmos. An angel explained to John the meaning of what John had seen in his vision.

> The beast that you saw was, and is not, and will ascend out of the bottomless pit and go to perdition. And those who dwell on the earth will marvel, whose names are not written in the Book of Life from the foundation of the world, when they see the beast that was, and is not, and yet is.
>
> Revelation 17: 8 (NKJV)

The world will marvel and be seduced with intrigue and flattery by this beast. According to the scripture, the one that will head up a one-world order is the Antichrist, and he will ascend out of the bottomless pit. When the people of the world begin to get comfortable with this vile man, he will begin to gain power and control over the globe. However, it is told of this vile man's destruction in the end:

> But the court will sit, and his power will be taken away and completely destroyed forever. Then the sovereignty, power, and greatness of all the kingdoms under heaven will be handed over to the holy people of the Most

High. His kingdom will be an everlasting kingdom, and all rulers will worship and obey him.

Daniel 7:26-27 (NIV)

According to this passage, we can be confident that in the end his power will be taken away and he will be destroyed forever. We can praise our God of the heavens that He will destroy this evil, and God's kingdom will last forever!

The apostle Paul encouraged the church at Thessalonica with these words:

> We are bound to thank God always for you, brethren, as it is fitting, because your faith grows exceedingly, and the love of every one of you all abounds toward each other, so that we ourselves boast of you among the churches of God for your patience and faith in all your persecutions and tribulations that you endure, which is manifest evidence of the righteous judgment of God, that you may be counted worthy of the kingdom of God, for which you also suffer; since it is a righteous thing with God to repay with tribulation those who trouble you, and to give you who are troubled rest with us when the Lord Je-

sus is revealed from heaven with His mighty
angels.

> 2 Thessalonians 1:3-7 (NKJV)

Paul is saying that God will give us patience and
faith through any persecution or tribulations that we
may endure. We will be counted worthy of the kingdom
of God for which we may suffer at the hands of this
world ruler in the end times.

> Beloved do not think it strange concerning
> the fiery trial which is to try you, as though
> some strange thing happened to you; but re-
> joice to the extent that you partake of Christ's
> sufferings, that when His glory is revealed,
> you may also be glad with exceeding joy.
>
> 1 Peter 4:12-13 (NKJV)

God promises rest to those who are troubled for the
sake of Christ. When the Lord Jesus is revealed from
heaven with His mighty angels, it will be worth it all.

CHAPTER 4

Weapons Prepared for the Battle of Armageddon

During the final stages of World War II, the United States, with the consent of the United Kingdom, dropped the first atom bomb over Hiroshima on August 6, 1945. Three days later, the United States dropped another atom bomb on Nagasaki, which brought the war to a close. Even though the war had ended, there was a cold war brewing in an arms race between Russia and the United States. The devil began to maneuver these two nations where they became fearful of each other. With each nation aware that they could be invaded by the other one with nuclear power, the taxes were raised to support the arms race and have continued to be raised until this present day. As we can see, Daniel talked about the raiser of taxes in verse Daniel 11:20, which could possibly be a person or a tax system that will be an overwhelming burden on the people. If it is a person, it could possibly be someone who rises to power and saturates the people with increased taxes. From verse 21 to verse 28, it describes the Antichrist, and there is no time gap between verse 21 and verse 28, which means whoever takes the place of the tax raiser will be the Antichrist. The other option would be a tax system that has been pressed upon the people because of the nuclear arms race. The Arms preparations have continued over the years for a potential World War III, which I believe will never happen! These weapons are being stockpiled, with the devil behind them, for the purpose of being used in the Battle of Armageddon. When Christ and His saints burst through the heavens to fight the battle of Armageddon, it will take heavy artillery on the part of the Antichrist and the false prophet. I cannot think of any other weapons they could launch into the atmosphere except nuclear artillery and missiles.

When a nation or a country prepares for war, it generally takes time to mobilize for the battle. During World War II, Japan bombed Pearl Harbor and caught the United States off guard because Japan had been preparing for several years to attack! We were not ready for them, but they were ready for us. It took two years before we could even make a dent in the way of aggression in stopping them. However, with God's favor and the strength of the United States, along with its allies, the war was won! The United States and other countries have been stockpiling nuclear weapons for years without understanding that these warheads are in reserve for the Battle of Armageddon. The Antichrist and the false prophet will already be mobilized as far as their nuclear system to fight the battle of Armageddon. The thirteenth chapter of the book of Revelation is devoted to describing the man of sin and all the indescribable vile things he will do after he comes into power. I will go into more detail later about the possible identity of the man that will rise to rule over the entire world government.

It is clearly stated below that Jesus will mount up on a white horse with the armies in heaven, which are clothed in white and clean linen, and they will follow Jesus on white horses.

> I saw heaven standing open and there before me was a white horse, whose rider is called Faithful and True. With justice, he judges and wages war. His eyes are like blazing fire, and on his head are many crowns. He has a name written on him that no one knows but he himself. He is dressed in a robe dipped in blood, and his name is the Word of God. The armies of heaven were following him, riding

on white horses and dressed in fine linen,
white and clean.

Revelation 19:11-14 (NIV)

Jesus and the believers, who have already been raptured, will gather together to fight the battle of Armageddon! Those who have accepted Jesus as their Savior and who have not taken the mark of the beast will
be engaged with Christ in this battle. According to
the nineteenth chapter of Revelation, Christ and His
bride win the battle, defeat the Antichrist and the false
prophet. These two are thrown into the lake of fire and
brimstone, where they will never again torment God's
people. The rest of them that received the mark of the
beast were killed with the sword that came out of the
mouth of Christ, and the birds gorged themselves on
the flesh of them. In chapter 20:1-3 (NIV), John saw an
angel coming down from heaven with a chain in his
hand. The angel seized the devil and bound him up and
cast him into the fire and brimstone for a thousand
years.

We can see in these scriptures that Christ conquers
and wins the battle of Armageddon. This battle will be
with the inhabitants of world empire number six, which
we have been describing. The importance of knowing
that we are living in world empire number five is rele-
vant to this battle simply because it will proceed the six

world empire. There is more than one place in the Bible that God speaks about the formation of world empire number five. God describes the world empire number five in Daniel chapter seven, chapter eleven, and also in Revelation chapter six and chapter thirteen. Many will argue the fact and say that "it's just a coincidence" that we have the Free World, the Communist World, and the Third World. I am confident that it is not a coincidence, dear readers. God has known this from the beginning, and out of His great love, He gave us symbols in the Word of God and foretold their origination and the way they would come to pass. He wanted us to understand where we are on His timetable, particularly at this point in time, and that we certainly are living today in world empire number five.

God shows us world empires in the form of metal symbols in Nebuchadnezzar's dream, with the exception of the clay feet. In the second chapter of Daniel, Nebuchadnezzar saw four symbols of world empires that were described from the head down but with no names. Later on, the angel told Daniel they were kings or kingdoms, but he did not indicate what kingdoms they might be. It's interesting that mankind named the Babylonian Empire, the Medio-Persian Empire, the Greek Empire, the Roman Empire, and men also named the Free World, the Communist World, and the Third World. People have had their hand in naming this three-way division that makes up empire number five and have used those terms for years, without recognizing that it comes straight out of the Word of God! Do you think that God would go to the trouble of foretelling the existence of the Babylonian Empire, the Medio-Persian Empire, the Greek Empire, and the Roman Empire and leave us in the dark about the fifth and sixth world empire? God intentionally took us from the first world empire straight through to the battle of Armageddon. He gave us symbols and numbers concerning this three-way division of the nations that constitutes world empire number five when they are collectively united. So I don't think there is room to argue that these world empires just "happened."

When Churchill gave that speech just after World War II, he was the first person that presented a symbol that started the time clock ticking and moving into the prophetic dream that Daniel had. His statement that a great iron curtain has been stretched from the Dardanelles to the Baltic established the Communist World. The Free World had already been established, and the Third World was in the making. All three of those symbols, the lion, the bear, and the leopard, found in the seventh chapter of Daniel, are all in a straight line preceding the fourth beast. The Antichrist will conquer the Free World, the Communist World, and the Third World. If he were to show up on the world scene now, he would not be able to conquer the Babylonian Empire, the Medio-Persian Empire, the Greek Empire, or the Roman Empire because those empires have already passed.

In Daniel 7:23-24, it mentions the beast will conquer three kings.

> He gave me this explanation: The fourth beast is a fourth kingdom that will appear on earth. It will be different from all the other kingdoms and will devour the whole earth, trampling it down and crushing it. The ten horns are ten kings who will arise from this kingdom. After them another king will arise, different from the earlier ones; he will subdue three kings.
>
> Daniel 7:23-24 (NIV)

The three kings in this passage are referring to the Free World, the Communist World, and the Third World. From the end of world empire number four, which was the Roman Empire, until right after World War II, there was a time-lapse in which we did not have a world empire on this planet. It is important to understand there is no time-lapse between world empire number five and world empire number six.

Let's confirm these world empires even further.

> The dragon stood on the shore of the sea. And I saw a beast coming out of the sea. It had ten horns and seven heads, with ten crowns on its horns, and on each head a blasphemous name. The beast I saw resembled a leopard, but had the feet like those of a bear and a mouth like that of a lion.
>
> Revelation 13:1-2 (NIV)

John saw a dragon standing on the sand of the sea, and he saw a beast rising up out of the sea, having ten horns and seven heads. It goes on to say that the beast resembled a leopard but had feet like those of a bear and a mouth like that of a lion. I want to call your attention to the first three symbols that Daniel saw in Daniel 7:4 (NIV), where he saw a lion, a bear, and a leopard. Notice they were all single animals and not three composed animals made into one. However, when we see the beast come up out of the sea in Revelation 13:1, the bear, the lion, and the leopard are combined into one. Now Daniel saw the Free World, the Communist World, and the Third World. What John saw was the three in one collectively, which places the entire world all under one government ruler. This is just one more confirmation of the three-way division of the current empire number five coming together under the rule of the Antichrist. I have taken great efforts to share multiple scriptures that support the idea that three empires, collectively, make up the fifth world empire. I don't mean to be repetitive, but it is important to understand that empire number six will follow empire five.

CHAPTER 5

The Four Horsemen

When John was in captivity on the island of Patmos, the Lord Jesus Christ came to John and gave to him the wonderful book of Revelation. When John was caught up in the spirit, he saw the four horsemen of the apocalypse. Over my father's lifetime, he had heard various interpretations of these four horsemen in Revelations 6:1-8, and he questioned if they have been interpreted correctly. I encourage you to take a moment and ponder the following interpretation of what these four horsemen could represent. This interpretation fits right into harmony with the flow of the Word of God in regards to where the world is currently and where the world is headed in the future. These four horsemen are symbolic of future events that will take place in the end times.

The first horse that John saw was a white horse, which had a rider on it. The rider wore a crown, carried a bow, and set out to conquer. This white horse is the same as the lion with eagle's wings that we saw in the seventh chapter of Daniel. It represents the nations that are known as the Free World. The United States of America is an example of the white horse. Teddy Roosevelt said, "We carry a big stick, but we speak softly." The nations that are considered the Free World are not aggressive nations that seek to take over other nations, to take away their liberty or any possessions they may have. They are considered free people and are doing everything in their power to see that everyone on the face of this earth is also a free person. The United States of America has always desired that people around the globe enjoy the same lifestyle that it has enjoyed for so many years. A man's heart was given to the United States of America from the time of its inception. What other country has the inscription "In God We Trust" written on their money? I believe that God Almighty had a hand in establishing America. As people migrated from other countries, they were amazed in wonderment at how this country was full of rich blessings, even the ungodly prospered. God told Abraham that there were many nations in his loins, and He made a promise to bless Abraham and to bless those nations through Abraham's seed.

Abram fell facedown, and God said to him, "As for me, this is my covenant with you: You will be the father of many nations. No longer will you be called Abram; your name will be Abraham, for I have made you a father of many nations. I will make you very fruitful; I will make nations of you, and kings will come from you. I will establish my covenant as an everlasting covenant between me and you and your descendants after you for the generations to come. The whole land of Canaan, where you now reside as a foreigner, I will give as an everlasting possession to you and your descendants after you; and I will be their God."

Genesis 17:3-8 (NIV)

God is fulfilling the promise from three thousand years ago, and it's not based on how good we are or how much we know. Even though the United States of America has experienced times of horrific racial and social injustice, a cruel civil war, and broken laws, they, along with other free countries, have been living in that promise ever since God's covenant with Abraham. With that in mind, you will see how the white horse fits perfectly as you continue to read this passage.

The next horse John saw was a red horse. When you think about all the nations and all of the countries in the world, what comes to your mind when you think of the color red? The color itself makes a statement! My father believed the red horse that John saw stood in his vision represented USSR. As I stated before, the Communist system opposed the liberty of religious freedom at that time in history. History tells us that approximately 105,300 clergymen were executed during the Great Purge. The next thing we see about the red horse is that it is given a great sword. After World War II, the Soviet Union government system demonstrated its attempt to take peace from the earth. The USSR government system collapsed in 1991.

The next horse we see in Revelation is a black horse. This horse will take a little more explaining and understanding. The rider on this horse had a pair of scales in his hands, and John heard this in the vision: "Then I heard what sounded like a voice among the four living creatures, saying, 'Two pounds of wheat for a day's wages, and six pounds of barley for a day's wages, and do not damage the oil and the wine!'" (Revelation 6:6, NIV) When we look at the inflation of this current age, it is the greatest that the world has ever known. Research tells us the value of the penny at that point in time, and the amount that went into a measure of wheat was enough to make a loaf of bread. This passage indicates that at the end of the age, a loaf of bread could cost a day's wages and that, my friends, is inflation! The passage goes on to warn us not to hurt the oil and the wine. Let's take a moment to look at the opaque nations and how they tie into this passage regarding the oil and the wine. For generations, the opaque nations, such as Saudi Arabia, Iraq, Iran, and Turkey, were wandering tribes who lived in tents and carried all their possessions with them as they moved about in the desert, from one oasis to another. In 1908 a large British cooperation struck the first big petroleum oil find in Iran. In the year 1938, several oil people in the USA and other parts of the western world began looking at the vast desert in Saudi Arabia, suspecting there may be oil over there. It took very little effort to get consent from these Arabic nations to allow the drilling for oil wells in that desert. In a short period of time, they discovered the biggest commercial oil deposits in the world!

In 1973 Arab members of the Organization of Petroleum Exporting Countries (OPEC) imposed an oil embargo against the United States, Canada, Japan, Netherlands, and the United Kingdom in retaliation against the United States for their decision to re-supply the Israel military. Shear panic began to set in, and people would rush to the gas stations before daybreak, where they would find vehicles lined up for blocks just to get about five gallons of gas. When the gas stations began to run out of gas, they would close their stations down until they could get more gas. Many times it would be three to four days before they would reopen again. It did not take long before the Arab nations recognized how much power they had in the oil. They quickly realized they could raise the price of oil per barrel and more than likely get it.

By the end of 1974, oil prices soared from $3.00 a barrel to $12.00 a barrel. Each time they raised the price of oil, it did not hurt the sales. The United States and other countries bought as much as they ever had, even when it soared to $42.00 per barrel. Inflation soared within the western world, and it all started with the oil issue. When John heard a voice saying, "Damage not the oil," I do not believe it was referring to the kind of oil that we fry our eggs with for breakfast. It was referring to the black crude oil that comes out of the ground.

The western culture depends on vast amounts of crude oil to maintain their lifestyle, such as operating a car, machinery, factories, beauty products, certain food products, and much more. Our economic future and the strength of our globe are at risk without an abundant supply of oil. In recent years, there has been talked of producing cleaner forms of energy and fading out the use of crude oil altogether. According to the voice command that John heard, there is a strong caution to avoid hurting the oil at all. Whether it comes through power and dominion from the other nations or eliminating oil altogether, it could be considered damaging the oil.

The black horse could certainly be referring to the inflation that most countries are experiencing, and it continues to grow at a rapid pace. When John heard the statement "Hurt not the oil and the wine," there was an example given of various products like wheat and barley. God was foretelling of what was to come, and He certainly was on target!

Let's take a look back to the book of Daniel in the seventh chapter where Daniel saw four beasts, and the third was like a leopard with four heads, four wings, and dominion is given unto it. Daniel was referring to the Third World, and it's the only symbol that had this statement attached to it, "And dominion shall be given unto it." Where does this dominion come from, and what will it have dominion over?

The opaque nations are not members of the Communist World, neither are they members of the Free World. After exploring the history of how inflation started with the oil embargo, it's not difficult to figure out where the dominion came from. It came from the abundance of crude oil and the power that it carried with it at that time in history. The oil has made them some of the most affluent of the Third World countries.

When inflation reaches its peak, there is a potential for global famine as Jesus spoke to us: "For nation will rise against nation, and kingdom against kingdom. And there will be famines, pestilences, and earthquakes in various places" (Matthew 24:7, NKJV). Right before Jesus descended into heavens to sit down at the right hand of His Father, He commissioned His disciples to go into all the world and preach the gospel. Thankfully, the gospel has been spread in all of the three world empires, the Free World, the Communist World, and the Third World.

The fourth horse that John saw in Revelation 6:8 was a pale horse.

> When the Lamb opened the fourth seal, I heard the voice of the fourth living creature say, "Come!" I looked, and there before me was a pale horse! Its rider was named Death, and Hades was following close behind him. They were given power over a fourth of the earth to kill by sword, famine and plague, and by the wild beasts of the earth.
>
> Revelation 6:7-8 (NIV)

This pale horse represents the kingdom of the Antichrist, who will head up a one-world government. This man will rule over the entire planet with a new world order, but he will need to conquer the Free World, the Communist World, and the Third world in order to assemble a one-world government system. Scripture says that death rides on this pale horse, and it has power over one-fourth of the people on earth to kill by the sword, famine, plague, and wild beasts!

I have pretty well covered the four symbolic horsemen: the white horse, the red horse, the black horse, and the pale horse. That gives us some insight into the world that we are living in right now, world empire number five. I recall my father saying that one of these days, the world is going to wake up, and the man of sin will be sitting on our doorstep! Even as I write this, he is preparing to orchestrate the new world order. He is going to stick his ugly head up, and when he does, these things that I am sharing with you will come to pass.

When we think about the great tribulation that will take place in the end times, it seems more comforting to believe that it will not include the believers. After all, who in the world would want to go through anything so horrific? There are different camps on the subject, with some believing that Christ will return before the great tribulation, and others believing the great tribulation will take place before Christ returns for His church. Others believe that Christ will return in the middle of the great tribulation. I would much rather lean into the idea of not going through the great tribulation at all! We will walk through several passages concerning the great tribulation to see what God revealed to Daniel and other biblical characters about the great tribulation. It is important to remember that Jesus promised that He will come back to get us, regardless of the time frame of the great tribulation. He will welcome us into our beautiful, magnificent home called heaven.

A few years ago my husband and I were excited to hear that a new superstore was having its grand opening ceremony! As we pulled up in the parking lot, we noticed a large stage with the City Mayor as the officiating host. As the ribbon-cutting was drawing near, I happened to notice the uniformed employees had suddenly disappeared into the store. My husband and I had guessed they were going directly to their checkout stands to prepare for their guests. As we entered the store, there were employees lined up on both sides of the aisle with a thunder of clapping, beautiful words of welcome, and warm smiles that melted our hearts. It continued for almost halfway to the back of the store. We eventually made a turn down a side aisle and stopped. It was an amazing spiritual experience for both of us, and as we turned to face each other, we realized that we both had tears in our eyes. Through trembling lips, I asked my husband these questions: "Do you think this is how it's going to be when we enter heaven?" "Will the angels be clapping with excitement to see us?" "Will they be lined up to escort us to the throne where our Father is waiting to welcome us?" My husband's reply was, "I think so, and even better." As believers in Jesus Christ look forward to His coming, we can be assured that He will welcome us into His kingdom with a great magnificent celebration! All sorrows will pass away when we enter the kingdom of heaven. There will be dancing, clapping, singing, and praising our God Almighty before the throne. He has been preparing to welcome us into heaven with the greatest celebration we could ever imagine!

CHAPTER 6

The Great Tribulation

In Daniel 7:25 (NIV), it says, "He will speak against the Most High and oppress his holy people and try to change the set times and the laws. The holy people will be delivered into his hands for a time, times and half a time." In Daniel's vision, he was told there was a time frame for this Antichrist to reign, which is three and half years. When it speaks of the holy people being delivered into his hands for a time, times, and half a time, it is referring to three and half years of persecution for the believers.

Who are these people who are delivered into the hands of this one world leader for three and half years? These people are the believers all over this world who proclaim the name of Christ and believe that He is the only one who died and rose again to save them from their sins. These are the believers in Jesus Christ, who acknowledge that he is the only Savior of the world. Jesus is the only name by which men can be saved and have eternal life. Acts 4:12 (NKJV): "Salvation is found in no one else, for there is no other name under heaven given to mankind by which we must be saved."

It will not be the wrath of God that they suffer, it will be the wrath of man, the Antichrist himself. The wrath of God is reserved for those who take the mark of the beast in their forehead or right hand and worship the Antichrist. When Jesus talked about the great tribulation in Matthew 24, Jesus intentionally used the term "the great tribulation." The people of God have suffered many tribulations over the centuries, but that is not to be confused with great tribulations, such as the world has never seen before. There is a staggering amount of Christians that have been persecuted and killed yearly, and the number is increasing on a daily basis. Under the rule of Communist leader Mao Zedong, between the years nineteen fifty-nine to nineteen sixty-one, it is estimated that over 45 million Chinese people were killed and approximately five hundred thousand of these were Christians. It is undeniable that scores of Christians have suffered tribulations over the years, but this great tribulation will be more horrific than mankind has ever experienced.

What does it mean in Revelation 6:8 when it says that its rider on the pale horse was named Death, and Hades was following close behind? We can understand that Death represents the Antichrist but who is this following right behind him? In the thirteenth chapter of Revelation, there is another beast that comes up after the first beast. This second beast is the false prophet, and he is going to introduce the entire world to a new and revolutionary economic system. This economic system will be different from anything that a man has ever experienced. This economic system will require a mark on the right hand or the forehead for the participants of this new world order. John was very clear about where the mark will be placed on a person's body. He clearly states the mark will be on the right hand or forehead. Without this mark, it will be impossible to buy or sell anything.

As we reflect over the past years on how our money system has slowly but surely changed, it has been like watching a movie in slow motion. It is easy to see how the mark of the beast could make its way into the economic system. We have gradually moved away from using cash, paper checks, and even banking in person. The experts at some point in time convinced the world that using credit cards, online banking, and direct deposit was the most convenient and sensible thing to do. However, there have been problems on a global level as a result of this technology payment system. There are banks and insurance companies that are paying millions and millions of dollars to cover identity theft, scams, hackers, and lost or stolen credit cards. It leads us to believe that this global technology economic system is not working as well as they proposed. It's certainly easy to see how we are being set up for a system that appears to be a simple and so-called "safer" system. By the time the idea of a mark on the right hand or forehead is introduced, the world will be easily convinced that this is the way to go! People by the billions will fall for such a system because they will already be conditioned for it. It will be nearly impossible to escape or hide any place because technology will have has such a state-of-the-art tracking device. I am thoroughly convinced that every person on the face of the earth will be easily known and easily located by the Antichrist and the false prophet.

In chapter twenty-four of the book of Matthew, Jesus tells of how brother will betray brother, children will rise up against their parents and cause them to be put to death, neighbor betraying neighbor in the end times. In this passage, Jesus is referring to the betrayal of loved ones under this new one-world system. These betrayals may even be something that is required once the Antichrist comes into power. He will convince millions of people of this new money system. He will seduce many to take the mark of the beast at the beginning of his powerful position. When a certain percentage of the population has this mark on their right hand or forehead, the man of sin will begin to put pressure on those who have refused to accept the mark. I need to stop here and offer a strong caution for anyone reading this book. In Revelation 14:9-10 (NKJV), it shouts a strong warning for us not to take the mark of the beast and not to worship the beast, nor its image.

> A third angel followed them and said in a loud voice, "If anyone worships the beast and his image, and receives his mark on his forehead or on his hand, he himself shall also drink of the wine of the wrath of God, which is poured out full strength into the cup of His indignation."
>
> Revelation 14:9-10 (NKJV)

This mark on the right hand or forehead is the devil's branding.

There will be millions of people who will be persecuted and even killed in the great tribulation. If we consider that we have over eight billion people on the face of this earth, and the Bible says that one-fourth of them will die for the sake of Christ, that means over two billion people will have been persecuted or put to death. In Revelation 6:9 (NIV), it says, "When he opened the fifth seal, I saw under the altar the souls of those who had been slain because of the Word of God and the testimony they had maintained."

There will be an army of people who will be persecuting the Christians, but they won't necessarily be in uniforms or carrying guns and ammunition. It will be an army of civilians that have willingly taken the mark of the beast, and the man of sin has completely taken them over. They will be subject to every command he gives them. He will convince the world that he is the true Messiah, the true God, and the only way we will have peace on earth is to get rid of anyone who names the name of Christ. This one world leader won't force people to take the mark on their right hand or their forehead, but he will use every resource at his disposal to break their will.

There is no need to fear the great tribulation if we are in Christ. In Matthew 10:19-20 (NKJV), Jesus encouraged His followers not to worry about what a man can do to us, "But when they deliver you up, do not worry about how or what you should speak. For it will be given to you in that hour what you should speak; for it is not you who speak, but the Spirit of your Father who speaks in you." In verses 28-31, Jesus said,

> And do not fear those who kill the body but cannot kill the soul. But rather fear Him who is able to destroy both soul and body in hell.

> Are not two sparrows sold for a copper coin?
> And not one of them falls to the ground apart
> from your Father's will. But the very hairs
> of your head are all numbered. Do not fear
> therefore; you are of more value than many
> sparrows.
>
> Matthew 10:28-31 (NKJV)

The only thing we are to fear is to deny Christ as the Savior of the world.

John saw a vision of those who came out of the great tribulation. There was a promise from God for those who had endured.

> Then one of the elders answered, saying to
> me, "Who are these arrayed in white robes,
> and where did they come from?" And I said
> to him, "Sir, you know." So he said to me,
> "These are the ones who come out of the great
> tribulation, and washed their robes and made
> them white in the blood of the lamb. There-
> fore, they are before the throne of God and
> serve him day and night in His temple. And
> He who sits on the throne will dwell among
> them. They shall neither hunger anymore nor
> thirst anymore; the sun shall not strike them,
> nor any heat; for the Lamb who is in the midst

of the throne will shepherd them and lead
them to living fountain of waters. And God
will wipe away every tear from their eyes."
Revelation 7:13-17 (NKJV)

God never promised that we would not suffer on this
earth, but He did promise us a place where we would
never suffer again.

Dear reader, now is the time to think upon these
things, now is the time to make a decision to be a
Christ-follower. I'm bringing these things to your attention because you may not have heard these things
from teachers or by reading a book. This information is
not to impose fear or intimidation of any kind. We have
no need to fear when we are in Christ because He will
give us everything we need during these testing trials.
This information is simply to make you aware and to be
alert! My desire is to point out the many passages in the
Bible that provide symbols, visions, and revelation that
give evidence of what to expect in the end times.

Many will tell you the Antichrist will only control the
country of Israel. The Bible is very clear that he will be
a world dictator and that he is the devil's own man, the
seed of Satan. As we look at the first verse of the thirteenth chapter of Revelation, it tells us where the beast
will arise from. It says the dragon (Satan) stood on the
shore of the sea, and John saw a beast coming up out of

the sea. This is the same beast that was mentioned by John in the seventeenth chapter of the book of Revelation. It says that this beast was, and is not, and shall ascend out of the bottomless pit and go into destruction, and the whole world will wonder and look upon him in amazement! They just can't believe that this man was once on the earth and then died, and here he is again on earth. The man of sin, the Antichrist, talked about in the thirteenth chapter of Revelation, has come out of the bottomless pit to do his deplorable work on earth.

In the midst of the great tribulation, the Lord will descend from heaven and gather His children home. Immediately following the Rapture of the church, the wrath of God will be poured out on those who rejected and cursed God.

There will be a war raged by Satan and his followers against Christ and His church. This war will be the battle of Armageddon that I mentioned earlier. Christ and His church win the battle, and Satan is cast into hell for one thousand years. After the one thousand years of peace on earth, the devil will be loosed for a short time to wage war against Christ, but Christ will cast the devil into the fire and brimstone, where the Antichrist and the false prophet are.

In John's vision, it says,

They are also seven kings. Five have fallen,
one is, the other has not yet come; but when
he does come, he must remain for only a little
while. The beast who once was, and now is
not, is an eighth king. He belongs to the seven
and is going to his destruction.

Revelation 17:10-11 (NIV)

What John saw was the Babylonian, Persian, Greece,
and Roman empires, which totals four, and when you
add the Free World, the Communist World, the Third
World, it adds up to seven, and the eighth is the one
world which will be governed by the Antichrist. John received this book during the reign of the Roman Empire.
When John saw the seven kings, and five had fallen,
there were only three that had fallen at that time, the
Babylonian Empire, the Medio-Persian Empire, and
the Greek Empire. Since that time, the Roman Empire
has fallen, which counts for four of the kings, and the
fifth king represents the empire that we are now currently living in, which will fall into the hands of the
eight king represented, the ruler of the new world order, the Antichrist.

As I stated before, the fifth world kingdom con-
sists of three heads of government, the Free World,
the Communist World, and the Third World countries.
So, we can conclude it takes seven kings to constitute

five world empires. With that in mind, we know that according to John's vision, this empire, too, will fall! The seventh and final world empire will be God's kingdom that will never be passed to another. The fact that Christ-followers will live in a kingdom that will never pass away should make every Christ-follower shout for joy! In Daniel 2:44, it says that in the day of these kings shall the God of heaven set up a kingdom that will never be destroyed.

> Do not let your hearts be troubled. You believe in God; believe also in me. My Father's house has many rooms; if that were not so, would I have told you that I am going there to prepare a place for you? And if I go and prepare a place for you, I will come back and take you to be with me that you also may be where I am.
>
> John 14:1-3 (NIV)

CHAPTER 7

The First Beast

I want to bring a thought to you that perhaps you have never heard before, and it may sound strange or even shocking to hear this thought. Again, I respect the ideas, theories, and revelations of others who may have a different view about the events surrounding the end times. When the Holy Spirit revealed these mysteries to my father in God's Word, I was taken back. My father did not expect anyone to accept the idea of the church going through the great tribulation. It is not a pleasant thought at all, but my father felt a responsibility to share his perception of what he believed to be true. It is extremely important to be aware of who is going to be in charge of the next world empire, or as it is often referred to as the one-world government. The Bible teaches that the devil has the powers to reproduce his seed in human form. Again, that may sound a little strange if you have never heard it before. Please stay with me as we look to the Word of God to support this idea.

We will start in chapter three of the book of Genesis, where Adam and Eve fell into sin in the Garden. God questioned Eve about eating the forbidden fruit in Genesis 3:13-15 (NKJV): "And the Lord God said to the woman, 'What is this you have done?' The woman said, 'The serpent deceived me, and I ate.'" At that point, God turned his attention to the serpent, which was actually the devil himself, in the form of a snake. God spoke directly to the devil in verse 15 and said, "And I will put enmity between you and the woman, And between your seed and her Seed; He shall bruise your head, And you shall bruise His heel." In the NIV translation, it says, "I will put enmity between you and the woman, and between your offspring and hers; he will crush your head, and you will strike his heel." When I read this, I had to ask myself this question, "What did God mean when He told the devil that he had a seed or offspring?" Does this mean the devil is married and has children? If the devil has a seed, does he have a Mrs. Devil somewhere, and they have a lot of little devils? No, I don't believe he does, but my father believed the devil had a seed that was planted within a person and was allowed to reproduce.

God's plan to redeem the lost seed of Adam was through Jesus Christ, who would leave the heavens and take upon Him the form of a man, who was born on this earth to a young virgin girl named Mary. Jesus was the offspring of God, the only begotten Son of the Father. God is a family, and all those who are born again in the spirit of God are His beautiful children of God.

> For in him we live and move and have our being. As some of your own poets have said, "We are his offspring." Therefore since we are God's offspring, we should not think that the divine being is like gold or silver or stone—an image made by human design and skill.
>
> Acts 17:28-29 (NIV)

When God used the term *"my seed"* in the Garden and in the same breath He said the *"seed of the woman,"* God was referring to Jesus because Jesus is not the seed of a man, He is the seed of God.

Just as God has a family, the devil also has a family. If the devil has a family, then who is his offspring, and how does this fit into the end times? The thought that an unnatural seed could be planted in the womb of a human woman, and produce a super-natural offspring, seems impossible.

If the devil has the ability to reproduce and have offspring, then is it possible that the devil could have a son? After all, the devil has tried to mimic God in every way possible, which includes the Trinity. We have God the Father, Jesus the Son, and the Holy Spirit. Could the devil have a counterfeit Trinity, which includes himself, the Antichrist, and the false prophet? God's plan was to send His Son into the world to save the world and to do the work of the Father. Could it be that the devil is sending his son into this world to do the work of his father, the devil? Is it possible the Antichrist is a son of the devil, and could the false prophet also be his offspring and a counterfeit of the Holy Spirit?

After Jesus descended into heaven to sit down at the right hand of the Father, the Holy Spirit was sent forth to carry out the work of the Father and the Son. Could it be that the false prophet will also be sent to carry out the work of the devil and the Antichrist?

> Then I saw a second beast coming up out of the earth. It had two horns like a lamb, but it spoke like a dragon. It exercised all the authority of the first beast on its behalf, and made the earth and its inhabitants worship the first beast, whose fatal wound had been healed.
>
> Revelation 13:11-12 (NIV)

Earlier I had mentioned that in Revelation 13:1, John saw a beast coming up out of the sea, and afterward, he saw another beast coming up out of the earth. When you read the description of the beast, it seems pretty convincing the first beast is the Antichrist which is the next world leader, and the second beast is the false prophet. I will expand on the second beast in the next chapter.

Every scripture and passage that my father studied about the Antichrist reveals that the finger of God perhaps points to one man, and his name is Judas Iscariot, the one who betrayed Jesus Christ. Please stay with me while I share the reason that my father came to that conclusion. In John 6:70-71 (NKJV), Jesus made a thought-provoking statement to His disciples. Jesus answered them and said, "'Did I not choose you, the twelve, and one of you is a devil?' He spoke of Judas Iscariot, the son of Simon, for it was he who would betray Him, being one of the twelve." Jesus did not say that Judas associates with devils, nor did he look like a devil. Jesus said that Judas is a devil! Later on, in John 17:12 (NKJV), Jesus was praying to the Father for His disciples, and He mentioned the son of perdition in His prayer: "While I was with them in the world, I kept them in your name. Those whom you gave Me, I have kept; and none of them is lost except the son of perdition, that the scripture might be fulfilled." The word perdition means someone who is unredeemable or eternally lost. This passage tells us a lot about how Jesus viewed Judas Iscariot. He referred to Judas as a devil, and He viewed Judas as eternally lost. Jesus did not say that Judas was of the devil, nor did He say that he acted like the devil. Jesus said that Judas is a devil! Jesus refers to Judas as the "son of perdition" in this passage, which means doomed to hell or destruction. There are no accounts in the Bible that God ever referred to anyone as the son of perdition, except Judas Iscariot.

If a person is a son, he certainly has a father, and if Judas is the son of perdition, who is his father? When God had that conversation with the devil in the Garden, God informed the devil that not only did God have a seed, but the devil also had a seed. God said that He would put enmity (hatred) between the devil's seed and God's seed.

In Matthew 26:24 (NKJV), Jesus made another statement about Judas Iscariot to His disciples while reclining at the table of the last supper. Jesus said, "The Son of Man indeed goes just as it is written of Him, but woe to that man by whom the Son of Man is betrayed! It would have been better for that man if he had not been born." Did Jesus say it was better if this man had never been born because He knew that Judas was going to betray Him? I personally don't think that is the reason Jesus made that statement. I think the reason Jesus made that statement was because Jesus knew that Judas was from a different seed.

Jesus did not die for devils, He died only for the seed of Adam. It would have been better if Judas had never been born because there was no way that he could ever be saved. This particular theory could sound judgmental of Judas Iscariot to most people, and it is never okay to label anyone as doomed to destruction because only God knows the ultimate future of each human soul. No matter how lost or evil a person may seem, we are to pray for his redemption. In 1 Timothy 2:1, it says that we are to pray and make intercession for all men, and in verse 4 it says that God desires for all men to be saved. We are never the judge of who is going to be lost or saved; however, Jesus said in John 17:12 (KJV) that of all of His disciples, none has been lost, except the son of perdition. God chose to reveal His plan of destruction for Judas, the son of perdition, to His disciples. This certainly looks like Judas was already doomed for destruction, according to this passage.

The apostle Paul refers to the Antichrist as the man of sin and the son of perdition in 2 Thessalonians 2:2-7 (NKJV). Paul is using labels that perhaps the church of Thessalonica had never heard before when he used the term, "man of sin" and "the son of perdition." In the same breathe that Paul refers to the man of sin, he also used the term "son of perdition." We recall that Jesus referred to Judas as the son of perdition in John 17:12, and now Paul is using the same title in reference to the Antichrist or the man of lawlessness. It is the same man talked about in Revelation 13:1-10, and also the same beast in Daniel 7:7 that had great iron teeth and brass claws that conquered three kingdoms. In my father's opinion, the man that is being referred to as the son of perdition, the beast, and the man of sin is the disciple who betrayed Jesus, Judas Iscariot.

Could it be possible that Judas Iscariot will convince people that it was really himself, and not Jesus, that was the real Messiah? When Jesus was laid in the tomb, there were those that were suspicious. Accusations were made that the disciples might steal His body and claim that Jesus was resurrected. Orders went out to increase the security guards around the tomb to prevent the disciples from stealing the body of Jesus. The son of perdition will imitate the resurrection and prove that he once walked on this earth, then died, and has come back to life. Please keep in mind the son of perdition will have an indestructible body, which can only be destroyed by God Himself in the end! What if Judas would appear on earth again and convince the Jewish leaders, and many others, that it was all a big mistake, and it was really himself that was the real Messiah who had come to bring peace, and that Jesus was a counterfeit? There are many people that do not believe that Jesus is the resurrected Messiah. If Judas can prove that he has been resurrected, that could be the convincing point. The beast who comes out of the bottomless pit will have been on the earth before as a human being. He died and went into hell and, at the appointed time, will be allowed to come out of the bottomless pit to take his place as ruler of the world empire number six. In Revelation 13:3 (NKJV), it states: "And I saw one of the heads as if it had been mortally wounded, and the wound had been healed." We recall how Judas fell headlong into his grave and no doubt had a mortal head wound. We can see how the devil imitates the death and the resurrection of Christ through the resurrection of the son of perdition.

It took my father years of intentional Bible study, fervent research, and guidance by the Holy Spirit to assemble this thought in his mind and in his spirit. I personally do not claim to be absolutely certain that Judas Iscariot is the Antichrist and that he is going to head up world empire number six, nor does the Bible name the Antichrist. There are many theories and ideas that have been circulating throughout the years about who the Antichrist will be, but in my opinion, this theory is the one that fits together more than any other theories that I have heard in my lifetime.

We know the Antichrist comes up out of the bottomless pit and shall go back into perdition in the end. In the nineteenth chapter of Revelation, the Antichrist and the false prophet are cast into a lake of fire and brimstone at the battle of Armageddon. The experts estimate the distance to the center of the earth is approximately 3,958 miles, and scientists report that the intensity of heat is about 10,800 Fahrenheit. I would imagine it is brimming with molting fire and brimstone. The earth is like a round tennis ball which makes it difficult to pinpoint the center and also makes it bottomless. If the bottomless pit went straight down vertically and would come out the other end, it wouldn't be bottomless.

The heart of the earth is hell, and this is where the Antichrist (the first beast) and the false prophet (the second beast) will descend from. The Antichrist and the false prophet will have bodies that are indestructible, as far as anyone having the ability to destroy them, except for God Himself, who does exactly that!

It's no wonder the whole world will wonder after the beast, a man who cannot be killed, has a body that can withstand fire and brimstone, performs signs and wonders, solves the world economic system, and has the power to rage war or make peace.

> The beast, which you saw, once was, now is not, and yet will come out of the Abyss and go to its destruction. The inhabitants of the earth whose names have not been written in the book of life from the creation of the world will be astonished when they see the beast,

because it once was, now is not, and yet will come.

Revelation 17:8 (NIV)

This passage talks about the world being astonished when they see the beast. The Bible says that what the Antichrist is doing, he will do and say before he and the false prophet are cast into the lake of fire. This beast is the man that will bring about the new world order (a one-world government). The Antichrist will open his mouth to blaspheme God, make war against the saints, and demand that every person denounce Jesus Christ and worship him. He will most likely make his entrance as a political or military figure who uses persuasive words and offers solutions for a troubled world. That is the beast that John saw coming up out of the sea. As I had mentioned, the Antichrist has different names, such as "the man of sin," "the son of perdition," and "the man of lawlessness." In Revelation, he is referred to as the first beast, but they are all the same person. The Antichrist will come out of the bottomless pit in an indestructible body, and he will head up world empire number six. He will be the devil's own man, and the devil will not surrender his power and seat of authority, except to his own seed. He will only transfer his power to his offspring, and only God Himself will be able to destroy the Antichrist, the false prophet, and the devil.

John saw in his vision a beast with a mouth that spoke proud words and blasphemies:

> The beast was given a mouth to utter proud words and blasphemies and to exercise its authority for forty- two months. It opened its mouth to blaspheme God, and to slander his name and his dwelling place and those who live in heaven. It was given power to wage war against God's holy people and to conquer them. And it was given authority over every tribe, people, language and nation. All inhabitants of the earth will worship the beast—all whose names have not been written in the Lamb's book of life, the Lamb who was slain from the creation of the world. Whoever has ears, let them hear. "If anyone is to go into captivity, into captivity they will go. If anyone is to be killed with the sword, with the sword they will be killed." This calls for patient endurance and faithfulness on the part of God's people.
>
> Revelation 13:5-10 (NIV)

Who are these people that the Antichrist wages war against? Who is John talking about? John is talking about God's faithful people that will suffer persecution during the great tribulation.

The Antichrist (son of perdition) will appear to be a good person who has come to resolve the multitude of problems in this world.

> And in his place shall arise a vile person, to whom they will not give the honor or royalty; but he shall come in peaceably, and seize the kingdom by intrigue. With the force of a flood they shall be swept away from before him and be broken, and also the prince of the covenant.
>
> Daniel 11:21-22 (NKJV)

And since he was here on earth before, and then was not, and now is, they will believe him. He will perform signs and wonder, and many will follow him, exalt him, and even worship him. All that is mentioned here will take place before the Rapture occurs.

God had to cast the devil and his angels out of heaven because the devil exalted himself with pride and wanted to be God himself. The devil has made every attempt to be God, but everything that he has tried has not worked, and his final attempt to show himself as God will be through the working of the Antichrist. We see in the book of Matthew the devil even tried to tempt

Jesus by telling Him that he would give Him all authority if Jesus would fall down and worship him.

> Again the devil took Him up on an exceedingly high mountain, and showed Him all the kingdoms of the world and their glory. And he said to Him, "All these things I will give You if You will fall down and worship me." Then Jesus said to him, "Away with you, Satan! For it is written, 'You shall worship the Lord your God, and Him only you shall serve.'"
>
> Matthew 4:8-10 (NKJV)

It is difficult to comprehend how the devil actually thought he could convince God Himself to fall down and worship him. The devil would have been overjoyed to transfer his authority into one man simply because the devil could get more accomplished through a human body. The devil is a spirit that we cannot see with our eyes, so his ultimate goal is to transfer all of his power and authority into a human body to dwell in, to carry out his evil deeds to God's people. His ultimate goal is to show himself to be God and to be worshipped by all mankind!

The good news is that in Revelation 20, John saw an angel come down from heaven carrying a great chain, and he bound Satan, cast him into the bottomless pit, and put a seal over it. Revelation 20:1-2 (NIV), "Then I saw an angel coming down from heaven, having the key to the bottomless pit and a great chain in his hand. He laid hold of the dragon, that serpent of old, who is the Devil and Satan, and bound him for a thousand years." The devil will remain in chains for 1000 years during the reign of the Prince of Peace, Jesus. After a thousand years, he will be released for a little time, but his end destruction will come with just one blast of fire from heavens. He will never again be able to accuse the brethren, deceive, manipulate or torment God's people, hallelujah!

CHAPTER 8

The Second Beast

The first beast that John saw in his vision came up out of the sea, but the second beast that John saw in Revelation chapter thirteen came up out of the earth. Revelation 13:11 (NIV), "Then I saw another beast coming up out of the earth, and he had two horns like a lamb and spoke like a dragon." This could mean there may be another door to hell that he will make his entrance from. We are going to spend a little extra time on the second beast simply because he is almost the spit and image of the Antichrist! You could almost say that he is the second Antichrist, in as much that he is the perfect likeness of the intentions of the first beast. The second beast is to be dreaded as much as the first beast with his superpowers to carry out every wicked plan of the first beast.

If Judas Iscariot is the seed and offspring of the devil, then who is this second beast that comes up out of the earth? This second beast that John saw is believed to be the false prophet. The second beast had two horns like a lamb, and he spoke like a dragon. This beast makes his entrance like a gentle lamb; however, at some point, he turns and speaks like a dragon. Horns usually represent domination and power, and since John saw that the second beast had two horns, it could possibly represent both the Antichrist and the false prophet. The false prophet could possibly be more of a religious leader rather than a political leader like the first beast. However, they both have the same identical agenda, which is to destroy God's people and exalt the Antichrist as God.

John's descriptive vision of the false prophet and the role he plays is very disturbing. When I study his behaviors and the hideous acts of violence toward God's people, my first inclination is to label him as the Antichrist instead of Judas Iscariot. However, because Jesus labeled Judas as the son of perdition and a devil, it causes me to look at another biblical character as the false prophet. Some have questions about the false prophet like: "Has he been here on earth before?" "Can we find this man anywhere else in the Bible?" "What will his role be in the end times?" My father began to ask the Lord for an understanding of who this false prophet could be because he felt it important for people to be aware of his identity, if at all possible.

John describes the false prophet and his role in the end times:

Then I saw another beast coming up out of the earth, and he had two horns like a lamb and spoke like a dragon. And he exercises all the authority of the first beast in his presence, and causes the earth and those who dwell in it to worship the first beast, whose deadly wound was healed. He performs great signs, so that he even makes fire come down from heaven on the earth in the sight of men. And he deceives those who dwell on the earth by those signs which he was granted to do in the sight of the beast, telling those who dwell on the earth to make an image to the beast who was wounded by the sword and lived. He was granted power to give breath to the image of the beast, that the image of the beast should both speak and cause as many as would not worship the image of the beast to be killed. He causes all, both small and great, rich and poor, free and slave, to receive a mark on their right hand or on their foreheads, and that no one may buy or sell except one who has the mark or the name of the beast, or the number of his name.

Here is wisdom. Let him who has understanding calculate the number of the beast, for it is the number of a man: His number is 666.

Revelation 13:11-18 (NKJV)

We can see in this passage the false prophet has all the authority of the first beast and plays a huge role in carrying out the commands given to him by the first beast. The Antichrist himself will simply give the commands, and the false prophet will willingly carry out every order, right down to every detail. Again we see the counterfeit in how the devil operates, such as God sent His son Jesus into the world and gave Him all authority. When the false prophet comes into this world, the Antichrist will give the false prophet all authority to carry out all of his evil intentions. The false prophet will cause people to make a mark on their right hand or forehead in order for them to buy or sell. In verse 13, it is very specific what part of the body the mark of the beast will be: "He causes all, both small and great, rich and poor to receive a mark on their right hand or on their foreheads." There has been speculation over the years as to what the mark will be. First of all, scripture tells us where it will be placed on our bodies; second of all, it will either be a mark, the name of the beast, or the number of his name.

> He causes all, both small and great, rich and
> poor, free and slave to receive a mark on their
> right hand or on their foreheads, and that no
> one may buy or sell except one who has the

mark, or the name of the beast, or the number of his name.

Revelation 13:15-17 (NKJV)

In verse 18, it tells us to calculate the number of the beast: "Here is wisdom. Let him who has understanding calculate the number of the beast, for it is the number of a man. His number is 666." In this passage, it almost sounds like the number 666 is a riddle and that we are to figure it out ourselves. In my perception, the number 666 ties into the fifth, sixth, and seventh world kingdoms. After processing the order of those world kingdoms and the significance placed on them, it is possible to calculate the meaning as being the number 665 could represent the fifth world kingdom simply because it contains the number five. The number 667 could represent God's kingdom because God's kingdom is number seven, and right down the middle is 666, which could represent the devil's one-world kingdom. This is something to ponder and perhaps consider when attempting to calculate the number of the beast. It places another significant emphasis on our awareness of the fifth world kingdom.

The false prophet will be the one who orchestrates the building of an image of the first beast, breathes life into it, and causes it to speak. I am not positive what the image of the beast will look like, but I have guessed that in this world of advanced technology, it could possibly be a gigantic computer network set up in the temple. The purpose of the image and its function are not clear, except for the purpose of worshipping the beast. The false prophet will demand that every person worship the image of the first beast. The image of the beast could possibly be created through technology through a satellite with the image of the Antichrist. Could it be that this technology will have the capability of tracking every single person on the face of the earth? After all, the beast will rule over the entire earth, and it makes sense that he would need to track every human being.

John's vision did not reveal the specific name of the second beast, but after my father sought for the answer in prayer, studying the Word of God, he was persuaded it is a biblical character named Esau, the twin brother of Jacob. As much as one studies and fervently researches, there is always a chance that a theory or an opinion may be off-target, but I will attempt to give you the reasons for my father's conclusion, and it is taken right out of the Word of God. God made the following statement about Esau and his twin brother Jacob. In Malachi 1:2, the Lord spoke through the prophet Malachi and said, "I loved Jacob, but Esau I hated."

I had mentioned that in Genesis 3:15, God talked to the serpent about the seed of the devil, and I have given reasons why the devil may have offspring. In that passage, God told the devil that He would put enmity between God's seed and the devil's seed. The word enmity means "hatred." In Malachi, we see that God used the term "hate" when God tells how He feels about Esau. It was many years after the Garden of Eden conversation that Esau was born. The world had been destroyed by the flood, and God grieved in His heart that He had ever made a man because the world had become so wicked. But not one time did God ever point His finger at any individual and say, "I hate him." In the time of Abraham and Lot, on the city of the plain, God burned the cities of Sodom and Gomorrah to a crisp because of their wickedness. However, God did not say He hated any of those individuals because of their wickedness. The word hate never came out of the mouth of God Almighty until we get to Esau.

Rebekah was the wife of Isaac and the mother of twin boys named Jacob and Esau. During the time that she was pregnant, she sensed that something unusual was going on inside of her womb. Rebekah was confused about why there was chaos going on inside of her. The babies jostled each other within her, so she asked the Lord why this was happening. In Genesis 25:22 (NKJV), The Lord responded to her and said, "Two nations are in your womb, and two peoples from within you will be separated; one will be stronger than the other, and the older one will serve the younger." Let's look at the biblical history of Esau and pursue an understanding of what God was saying to Rebekah.

The Lord declared:

> "I have loved you," says the Lord. "Yet you say, 'In what way have you loved us?' 'Was not Esau Jacob's brother'?" Says the Lord. "Yet Jacob I have loved; but Esau I have hated, And laid waste his mountains and his heritage For the jackals of the wilderness." Even though Edom has said, "We have the people been impoverished, But we will return and build up the desolate places," Thus says the Lord of hosts: "They may build, but I will throw down; They shall be called the Territory of Wickedness, And the people against whom the Lord will have indignation forever. Your eyes shall see, And you shall say, 'The Lord is magnified beyond the border of Israel.'"
>
> Malachi 1:2-5 (NKJV)

This passage mentions the territory of Edom and God's intentions toward the land of Edom. Even though Edom was a territorial space of land, the very name of Esau means Edom! In these passages of scripture, we see where God expressed how He felt about Esau. God said that He hated Esau, and the territorial space of

Edom would be called the Territory of Wickedness. We see in God's Word that God hates wickedness, but He does not single out an individual and say that He hates that person, except Esau. Could it be that perhaps Esau was not God's creation, which gave Him reason to hate him?

When twins are born, they usually look somewhat alike. This was not the case with Jacob and Esau because they looked quite the opposite. The writer of Genesis put an emphasis on how different these twin boys looked by using descriptive language. Esau was hairy all over, with red skin, and a rugged outdoor hunter who was favored by his father, Isaac. Jacob, in contrast, was a plain man, content to stay home and dwell in tents, favored by his mother. According to God's Word, there were two different manners of people in Rebekah's womb, and they would be separated into two different nations.

It was customary for the firstborn to inherit the birthright and the blessing from their father. Esau was born first from the womb and was entitled to the birthright and the blessing of Isaac. He was also entitled to all of Isaac's wealth, which Isaac inherited from his father, Abraham.

The Bible indicates that Esau placed no value on his birthright. In fact, it says that Esau despised his birthright, and he sold his birthright to his twin brother Jacob. When Isaac was old and blind, knowing that his end was near, he asked his son Esau to kill a deer and make a stew that he liked and to bring it to him. Rebekah overheard the conversation, and with urgency she told Jacob to hurry and kill a goat so that she could make a stew that Jacob could serve to his father, Isaac. I have questioned Rebekah's immediate reaction as to why a mother would be so desperate for a son to go after the birthright blessing. Why would a mother go to the point of urging her son to deceive his own father? Why did the thought of Esau inheriting the birthright blessing send Rebekah into a tailspin of sheer panic? Did Rebekah know there was something about Esau that was very different? Perhaps Rebekah sensed that perhaps Esau was a different manner of seed. Did Rebekah recall what God had said to her about there being two different nations of people in her womb? Did Rebekah sense that Jacob's precious linage was threatened and that it was urgent that she protect what would later become the Israelites, whom God adored, and still does to this day? After all, God had already told Rebekah that the older would serve the younger.

When Esau came in from the open country, he smelled the stew that Jacob had made, and he asked Jacob to give him some of it. Esau was dramatic when he told Jacob that he was going to die if Jacob would not give him some of his stew and that his birthright would be of no value if he was going to die anyway. Jacob responded to Esau by asking him if he would sell his birthright for some of the stew. Esau agreed that he would sell his birthright to Jacob for the stew.

In my father's perception, when God told the serpent in the very beginning of Genesis that He would put enmity between the devil's seed and the woman's seed, it began right here with these twin boys. There were two seeds in Rebekah's womb (two nations, two manners of people). My father was pressed to believe that Jacob was Isaac's seed, and Esau was the devil's seed. It makes you wonder if that might be the reason that Esau despised his birthright.

When Jacob brought the stew to his father, Isaac blessed Jacob by telling him:

> "Ah, the smell of my son is like the smell of a field that the Lord has blessed. May God give you heaven's dew and earth's richness—an abundance of grain and new wine. May nations serve you and peoples bow down to you. Be lord over your brothers, and may the sons of your mother bow down to you. May those who curse you be cursed and those who bless you be blessed."
>
> Genesis 27:27-29 (NIV)

A short time later, Esau came to his father Isaac with some stew that he had made and begged his father for a blessing. Isaac responded to Esau:

> His father Isaac answered him, "Your dwelling will be away from the earth's richness, away from the dew of heaven above. You will live by the sword and you will serve your brother. But when you grow restless, you will throw his yoke from off your neck."
>
> Genesis 27:39-40 (NIV)

As we can see, the blessing that Isaac gave Esau was quite the opposite of the blessing that he gave Isaac. As we follow Esau's life, it is very clear to see how he lived by the sword.

Sometime after Isaac blessed Jacob, he gave Jacob an important command:

> So Isaac called for Jacob and blessed him. Then he commanded him, "Do not marry a Canaanite woman. Go at once to Paddan Aram, to the house of your mother's father Bethuel. Take a wife for yourself there from among the daughters of Laban, your mother's brother."
>
> Genesis 28:1-2 (NIV)

When Isaac told Jacob to "go at once," I interpret that as being somewhat urgent! Could it be that Isaac's concern was that if Jacob prolonged his decision to take a wife that he might be tempted to take a wife from Canaan and nullify God's blessing? Some of the Canaanites were known for worshipping and acknowledging deities such as Baal and Asherah, and Isaac knew it!

Isaac blessed Jacob and told him that his life would be fruitful and multiply and that his descendants would inherit the land. When Esau saw that Jacob obeyed his father Isaac and went to Laban and took a wife there, Esau did exactly the opposite of Jacob! When he saw that the daughters of Canaan were not pleasing to his father, Isaac, he intentionally went to Canaan to his uncle's home and took Mahalath for a wife.

Esau was the father of the territory called Edom, and his descendants settled there. In Genesis 36:9 (NIV), it says, "This is the account of the family line of Esau the father of the Edomites in the hill country of Seir." The Edomites were fierce enemies of God's precious people, the Israelites. They practiced idolatry, and they worshipped other gods. Throughout Esau's lineage, you will see how conflicted the Edomites were with the Israelites. As we take a deeper look at the lineage of Esau, we will begin to understand how this all fits together with the end times.

If there is a probability that Esau was offspring of the devil, could it be that the unnatural seed was planted in Rebekah's womb? If so, I would like to suggest to you that Esau was most likely unaware of it. However, God knew it, and the devil knew it! Keep in mind that we saw in Genesis that God told the devil (in the form of a serpent) that he had a seed (offspring). According to Genesis 3:15 (NKJV), God told the serpent: "And I will put enmity between you and the woman, and between your seed and her Seed; He shall bruise your head, And you shall bruise His heel." In the NIV translation, it says, "And I will put enmity between you and the woman, and between your offspring and hers." According to this passage, we know that God has a seed, and the devil has a seed. We understand that God's seed was planted in Mary's womb (the woman's seed), and from that seed, which was planted by the Holy Spirit, came our Savior, Jesus Christ. God made it very clear that the devil also had a seed, and God had put hatred between His seed and the devil's seed.

If you follow Jacob's seed through the ages, you will see the salvation of the Lord. If you follow Esau's seed, you will see violence, wicked behavior, rebellion against God, and horrific belief systems. Jacob and his descendants are not only blessed by God over and over again in the Old Testament but also are mentioned numerous times in the New Testament. Matthew 8:11 (NKJV):

"And I say to you that many will come from the east and west, and sit down with Abraham, Isaac, and Jacob in the kingdom of heaven." Acts 3:13 (NKJV): "The God of Abraham, Isaac, and Jacob, the God of our fathers, glorified His servant Jesus, whom you delivered up and denied in the presence of Pilate, when he was determined to let Him go."

Let me take you to the book of Exodus to look at some of these wicked behaviors of Esau's lineage. The Hebrew word Edom means "red," which is the description of Esau at birth. Keep in mind that when Esau was born, he was red and hairy all over. The territory of Edom means "red dirt" since Esau came out of the womb, like a hairy garment and red all over. Much of the region that was considered Edom was covered with red dirt. The Edomites were descendants of Esau, and they used violence against God's beautiful people, the Israelites. In Genesis 36:12, it tells us that Esau had a grandson named Amalek. Amalek grew up in Esau's household and no doubt inherited Esau's intense deep hatred and jealousy for Jacob's descendants through the years. His offspring became the nation of Amalek, and they lived south of Israel. In Exodus 17:8-16, the Amalekites, descendants of Amalek, were the first nation to attack the Israelites as they had been released from Egypt's slavery and were on their way to the Promised Land. They were recovering from the weary escape from Pharaoh and had stopped at a desert wasteland called Rephidim. They were thirsting and were desperate for water, and out of God's loving compassion for His people, God had Moses strike a rock, and water gushed forth for the Israelites to drink. At a time when the Israelites were the most vulnerable, and while they were refreshing themselves, Amalek (Esau's grandson) attacked the Israelite's, making war against them in the wilderness. God did not take that attack on His precious people lightly. Amalek and the Amalekites were seen as the arch-enemy of God's people. Joshua was ordered by Moses to lead Israel into battle against Esau's descendants. God told Moses to tell Joshua to choose their choice of men and go out to exterminate the entire tribe of Amalekites. The Israelites won the battle against the Amalek's treacherous attack, killing their strongest warriors and then releasing the others to return home. Let's look at what the Lord told Moses about Amalek:

Then the Lord said to Moses, "Write this for a memorial in the book and recount it in the hearing of Joshua, that I will utterly blot out the remembrance of Amalek from under heaven." And Moses built an altar and called its name, The-Lord-Is-My-Banner; for he said, "Because the Lord has sworn: the Lord will have war with Amalek from generation to generation."

Exodus 17:14-16 (NKJV)

According to this passage, God will not forget what Esau's grandson did to the Israelites, even until the very end of time.

The writer of the book of Hebrews describes Esau as godless.

> See that no one is sexually immoral, or is god-less like Esau, who for a single meal sold his inheritance rights as the oldest son. Afterward, as you know, when he wanted to inherit this blessing, he was rejected. Even though he sought the blessing with tears, he could not change what he had done.

Hebrews 12:16-17 (NIV)

There are many accounts of where the descendants of Esau have abused, mistreated, and aggressively attempted to destroy God's precious people. Here are a few examples:

1. When the Israelites were camped in the desert, they were viciously attacked by the Amalekites disguised as the Canaanites.

2. When Moses pleaded with the king of Edom to let the Israelites pass through their land, promising not to touch their fields, drink their water, or touch their vineyards, the King of Edom cold-heartedly refused them passage.

3. In 1 Samuel, we read where the Amalekites invaded the town of Ziklag, burned it down, and kidnapped the women and children. David and his army hunted down the Amalekites, attacked them, and rescued all the women and children.

4. Out of King Agag's lineage came the wicked man Haman, who plotted to annihilate the precious Jewish people.

5. Out of Haman's lineage came King Herod, who sought out the baby Jesus and had planned to kill the Savior of the world, even to the point of killing all the male babies in Bethlehem.

Balaam the prophet spoke of Amalek in Numbers 24:20 (ESV) and said, "Then he looked on Amalek and took up his discourse and said, 'Amalek was the first among the nations, but its end is utter destruction.'" Balaam's prophetic message tells us that Esau's end is destruction. Now, I can't say that this is a popular thought or even a reasonable one, considering that God is a compassionate God toward His creation. But, what if Esau is not his creation? What if he is from a different seed? It is interesting to note that every time the Israelites would backslide, worship other gods, and rebel against God, God was quick to forgive and restore. However, not one time in the Bible can you find that kind of invitation to any of the descendants of Esau.

Samuel the prophet anointed Saul to be the first king of Israel and spoke to Saul the words that God had given him to speak. Samuel told Saul that God said to go and fight against the Amalekites and not to have pity on them.

> Thus says the Lord of hosts: "I will punish Amalek for what he did to Israel, how he ambushed him on the way when he came up from Egypt. Now go and attack Amalek, and utterly destroy all that they have, and do not spare them. But kill both man and woman, infant and nursing child, ox and sheep, camel and donkey."
>
> 1 Samuel 15:2-3 (NKJV)

Saul did what Samuel told him to do and went up and fought against the Amalekites. God's instruction was for Saul to kill everyone, which included women, children, even the little suckling's on their bed, the camels, their cattle, their sheep, their donkeys, and everything that breathed. The next day Saul went out to battle the Amalekites, and Saul won the battle. He killed every one of them, except King Agag and a few of the best animals. Samuel the prophet approached Saul after the battle was over, and Saul told Samuel, "I have done what the Lord had asked me to do." While they were yet speaking, Samuel asked Saul, "Why do I hear the sound of sheep and cattle?" Saul began to make excuses and said that he had kept the animals to sacrifice to God and that he was afraid of his army, so he listened to them instead of God. Samuel confronted Saul and told him that because he had been disobedient to God, his kingdom would be taken away from him and that he would no longer be king of Israel. Samuel went from there and searched for King Agag to kill him. How do we justify a command from a God of love and mercy to kill a whole tribe of people? God is a just and loving God who never does anything wrong! He has never done anything the way the devil does it, and if He did, He would be as guilty as the devil. Everything that God does is right because He is righteous and holy. Could it be that God knew that these people were not from God's seed; therefore, He pronounced righteous judgment on them? Psalm 137:7 (NIV), "Remember, Lord, what the Edomites did on the day Jerusalem fell. 'Tear it down,' they cried, 'Tear it down to its foundations!' God knew that for generations to come, the descendants of Esau would do wicked things to God's precious people.

Of course, that was not the end of the Amalekites and the remnant of Agag. They survived, regrouped, and were spread elsewhere. One of Esau's descendants was Haman, the son of Hammedatha, of the Royal blood of Amalek, who was the grandson of Esau. God used Queen Esther to spoil the plot of wicked Haman, the Amalekite, who schemed a plan to wipe out all of the precious Jewish people. Looking at the historical timeline, it is so interesting how enmity (hatred) between Esau and Jacob festered down through several generations. When wicked Hamen was hung, his ten sons were also slain with him. Could it be possible that Esau could make his appearance on the world scene again and take his place as the false prophet?

It is interesting to note that King Herod the Great was also a descendant of Esau, and according to history, King Herod was half Idumaean, and his father was by descent an Edomite. The Idumaeans were considered to be descendants of Esau. During King Herod's rule of Judea, he bore the title of King of the Jews, even though he was a Jew in name only. Herod's tyrannical rule over the Jews consisted of the savage murder of his own family members to maintain power and control. Herod's paranoia and murderess character rose up when he learned from the wise men of the east that another King of Jews had been born. When he had no success in finding the baby Jesus, he decided to have all the male children, two years and younger, put to death in Bethlehem.

Once again, we see a descendant of Esau trying to eradicate God's chosen people, even the Savior of the world! Herod could have been the last descendant of Esau, the Bible doesn't say. Let's take a look at a few more places in Bible that mention Esau and his final destruction! In Ezekiel 35:1-15 (NIV), a prophetic word went out from the Prophet Ezekiel to Mount Seir and all of Edom. The entire chapter is about God's intentions to destroy Mount Seir and Edom.

> Because you harbored an ancient hostility and delivered the Israelites over to the sword at the time of their calamity, the time their punishment reached its climax, therefore as surely as I live, declares the Sovereign Lord, I will give you over to bloodshed and it will pursue you. Since you did not hate bloodshed, bloodshed will pursue you.
>
> Ezekiel 35:5-6 (NIV)

In verses 14-15, it says,

> This is what the Sovereign Lord says: "While the whole earth rejoices, I will make you desolate. Because you rejoiced when the inheri-

tance of Israel became desolate, that is how
I will treat you. You will be desolate, Mount
Seir, you and all of Edom. Then they will
know that I am the Lord."

Ezekiel 35:14-15 (NIV)

God will always fight for Israel, and anyone who
comes against the precious people of Israel will answer
to God. We are to pray fervently for the peace of Jerusalem as it says in Psalm 122:6-7 (NIV), "Pray for the peace
of Jerusalem: 'May those who love you be secure. May
there be peace within your walls and security within
your citadels.'"

I recently have been reading through the book of Exodus in the Old Testament, and I find it interesting that
the attempt to rid the Jews goes as far back as the time
of Moses. Pharaoh made slaves out of the Israelites and
burdened them with ruthless, harsh labor. The Pharaoh
decided there were too many Israelites, so he ordered
all the Hebrew newborn male babies to be killed by the
midwives during childbirth. God spared the baby Moses, and the Hebrew lineage continued. We can see how
down through the ages, the enemy has tried to destroy
Jewish people. From Pharaoh to Esau, Amalek, wicked
Haman, Herod, and Hitler. However, God has promised that He will deliver Jewish people from the hands
of their enemies. God told the prophet:

"I will surely gather all of you. Jacob; I will surely bring together the remnant of Israel. I will bring them together like sheep in a pen, like a flock in its pasture; the place will throng with people. The One who breaks open the way will go up before them; they will break through the gate and go out. Their King will pass through before them, the Lord at their head."

Micah 2:12-13 (NIV)

In the second chapter of Daniel, the great statue that Nebuchadnezzar saw in his dream had feet and toes that were made of part iron and of part clay, and they mingled with the seed of men, but they did not adhere to one another. I believe the iron and the clay represent the sixth world empire set up by the Antichrist and the false prophet. It is interesting to note that these symbols of iron and clay mingle with the seed of men but could not adhere to them. In Daniel chapter seven, Daniel saw a beast that had large teeth made of iron. The iron represents the Antichrist and his brutal rule, and the clay represents the false prophet. These two beasts did not adhere to the seed of people, just like iron and clay to not cling to each other. There was a great stone that was cut out of the mountain without hands that struck the image in its feet and destroyed it. God strikes the world empire number six, and by doing so, He destroys all the other empires.

> And in the days of these kings the God of heaven will set up a kingdom which shall never be destroyed; and the kingdom shall not be left to other people; it shall break in pieces and consume all these kingdoms, and it shall stand forever.
>
> Daniel 2:44 (NKJV)

The statement about the great stone being cut out of the mountain without hands is symbolic of Christ. Christ will set up a kingdom that will never be destroyed.

There are people that are highly educated about the end times; however, some have literally stumbled over this truth for hundreds of years. This message is not always received with a positive response, but I believe that when the time is right and in God's timetable, it will be received.

I encourage you to take time to read the book of Obadiah in the Old Testament. Obadiah had a vision from the Lord, and the Lord told Obadiah that it was concerning Esau. Let me take you to the book of Obadiah and see what the prophet said about Esau. The book of Obadiah is only one chapter with twenty-one verses, but it mentions Edom twice and Esau seven times.

"But on Mount Zion there shall be deliverance, And there shall be holiness; The house of Jacob shall possess their possessions. The house of Jacob shall be a fire, And the house of Joseph a flame; But the house of Esau shall be stubble; They shall kindle them and devour them, And no survivor shall remain of the house of Esau," For the Lord has spoken.

Obadiah 17-18 (NKJV)

The Lord mentions that Esau will be stubble at the end of his time. Jacob will be a fire that kindles against Esau, and Esau's seed will be destroyed forever. I believe Obadiah's vision is showing us how Esau will be destroyed by fire and brimstone in the end time. God Himself will dispose of the devil's seed with fire.

There is another passage in Romans 9:6-23 (NKJV) that mentions Esau and Jacob. The apostle Paul pretty much devotes the entire chapter telling of the difference between Jacob and Esau. Paul explains that those who are of Abraham's seed are children of promise, but those of the flesh are not the children of God. Beginning in verse 10, Paul talks about the birth of Jacob and Esau:

And not only this, but when Rebecca also had conceived by one man, even by our father

Isaac, (for the children not yet being born, nor having done any good or evil, that the purpose of God according to election might stand, not of works but of Him who calls), it was said to her, "The older shall serve the younger." As it is written, "Jacob I have loved, but Esau I have hated."

Romans 9:10-13 (NKJV)

In verses 21-23, Paul describes the potter with a great chunk of clay in his hand and that the potter has the power over the clay to make one vessel of honor and another to dishonor:

Does not the potter have power over the clay, from the same lump to make one vessel for honor and another for dishonor? What if God, wanting to show His wrath and to make His power known, endured with much long-suffering the vessels of wrath prepared for destruction, and that He might make known the riches of His glory on the vessels of mercy, which He had prepared beforehand for glory.

Romans 9:21-23 (NKJV)

In our human understanding, it would be difficult to understand why God would choose to bear long-suffering the vessels of wrath, the vessels of disobedience that are doomed for destruction.

Paul said it was for the glory and mercy of God so that it might break forth to glorify the vessels that were created to be glorified. Paul was talking about the seed of God Almighty, which is His church, through Jesus Christ. Paul may have been referring to the Antichrist and the false prophet as the vessels of dishonor and the body of Christ as the vessels of honor.

Over the years, there have been many theories about who the Antichrist and the false prophet will be. I have mentioned my father's thoughts about the identity of the Antichrist as being Judas Iscariot and the false prophet as being Esau. There have been many people that have speculated that these characters could possibly be Nebuchadnezzar, the Pope, Hitler, or even a President of the United States. My father was convinced and sincerely believed, the Antichrist and the false prophet will be biblical characters.

Dear reader, we have no reason to fear these things because we have hope and rich inheritance waiting for us. The apostle Paul put it this way: "I pray that the eyes of your heart may be enlightened in order that you may know the hope to which he has called you, the riches of his glorious inheritance in his holy people" (Ephesians 1:18, NIV). There is not a definite time element mentioned in the Bible of when these prophetic events are

to take place. There have been many times through history that man has attempted to predict the time frame
for these things to come to pass. It may be generation
a far off, or it may not be, but it is important to make
sure our lives stay focused on Jesus and not live in fear
as we wait for His return. Jesus said in Matthew 25:13
(NIV), "Therefore keep watch, because you do not know
the day or the hour."

CHAPTER 9

The Abomination of Desolation

In Revelation 13:1 (NIV), John saw a vision of a beast that had seven heads and ten horns: "The dragon stood on the shore of the sea. And I saw a beast coming out of the sea. It had ten horns and seven heads, with ten crowns on its horns, and each head a blasphemous name." The ten horns are ten kingdoms that will partner with the Antichrist for a one-world government.

"The ten horns you saw are ten kings who have not yet received a kingdom, but who for one hour will receive authority as kings along with the beast. They have one purpose and will give their power and authority over to the beast. They will rage war against the Lamb, but the Lamb will triumph over them because He is the Lord of lords and King of kings—

and with him will be his called, chosen and
faithful followers."

Revelation 17:12-14 (NIV)

It is interesting that Daniel also saw ten horns in
Daniel 7:24 (NIV), which says, "The ten horns are ten
kings who will come from this kingdom. After them,
another king will arise, different from the earlier ones;
he will subdue three kings." The ten horns that Daniel
saw represent ten world's government leaders. At that
point in time, the seed of the devil will already be in the
world, and when the beast takes his seat of authority,
he will have these ten kingdoms convinced by flattery to
align with him for a one-world government. This passage brings clarity about who makes an alliance with
the beast and who they declare war on. These ten government powers will partner with the beast and wage
war against Christ and His church.

When we think about ten of the world's most prominent leaders in total alliance and agreement with the
Antichrist, the question arises, "What ties them together to this man of sin, and what causes them to make a
global mutual alliance?" As the world grows darker, the
inhabitants of the globe will be looking for solutions to
the chaos, broken economy, poverty, climate control,
violence, wars, and many other complex issues. This
will set the stage for the starting point of the beginning

of this man of sin taking over the whole planet. He will not necessarily have an army because it says in Daniel chapter eleven that he seduces these world leaders with flattery. He will also be able to perform great miracles, and he will have an indestructible body. After he establishes the one-world order, he will give orders to perform horrific devastation to God's people through the power that he gives the false prophet. God did not specifically reveal who the Antichrist and the false prophet will be; however, biblical history gives us an idea of who these men are, where they came from and where they will set up their place of authority. When these things have come to pass, we will eventually see the fury of the Antichrist and the false prophet unleashed upon those who even dare to breathe the name of Jesus.

In the ninth chapter of Daniel, it tells about how the children of Israel were in captivity in Babylon for seventy years, and God positioned Daniel in the midst of this to reveal many things about the end times. Daniel was a dedicated man of prayer, and God gave him visions and dreams concerning what was yet to come. Daniel was God's chosen vessel to interpret these visions and dreams through the power of God.

Daniel had a vision about seventy weeks, seventy years, and seventy weeks of years. If you add them all up, they total 490 years. At that point in time and right up until Christ was crucified, sixty-nine of those seventy weeks had been fulfilled. At the end of the sixty-ninth seven, the time clock stood still, and there is one more seven weeks (which is seven years) period left until all that was prophesied in this chapter is fulfilled under the seventy weeks. They will be fulfilled under the last seven years of this disposition before we enter into the 1000 years of Christ's reign here on the earth.

When Jesus, the Savior of the world, came to earth to seek and save the lost, He was rejected as the Messiah by many of the Jews, His own people. John 1:11-12 (NKJV): "He came to His own, and His own did not receive Him. But as many that received Him, to them He gave the right to become children of God, to those who believe in His name." Of course, there were many that did accept Jesus as the Savior of the world, including His disciples. There were many that received Him, and there were conversions to Christianity by the Jews in the early church. There are many Jewish people that are still anticipating the coming of their Messiah. Up to this current time, there are many Jewish people who have not accepted Jesus as their Messiah. However, there are thousands of Messianic Jews who still practice Jewish traditions and at the same time do acknowledge Jesus as the only Savior of the world. When this one-world leader appears on the world scene, Jewish people will be vulnerable to look to him as the anticipated Messiah who will bring peace and restore the daily sacrifices.

It seems to make sense that since the Jews will make a seven-year covenant with one who promises the restoration of the temple, which was destroyed in AD 70, and the restoring of the daily sacrifices, it would need to be someone who they recognize as a biblical character. I do not believe the Jews will settle on anyone as being their Messiah unless it is a biblical character and can give evidence that they were here before. This one-world leader has something they have been looking for, and they have something this leader needs from them. He will not take what he wants through force or battle, and he will conquer the world without an army. He will seduce, charm, and deceitfully try to convince the Jews that he is the true Messiah that they have been waiting for.

This one-world leader will be so convincing that the precious Jewish people will begin to partially accept the idea that he just might be their Messiah. However, there remains a shroud of doubt in their minds, and the Bible does not make it exactly clear why they are not totally convinced that He is the Messiah. This one-world leader will promise peace and a restoration of the daily sacrifices. His charm and flattery will draw the Jewish leaders in making a seven-year covenant with him.

> He will confirm a covenant with many for
> one seven. In the middle of the seven he will

put an end to sacrifice and offering. And at the temple he will set up an abomination that causes desolation, until the end that is decreed is poured out on him.

Daniel 9:27 (NIV)

The Jewish leaders agree to a seven-year covenant and make an agreement with him. However, there are some expectations and conditions to the covenant. If he meets those expectations in that seven-year period, they will proclaim him as their Messiah. If he does not meet those expectations, it's a deal-breaker! One of those expectations is that he re-establish the Jewish Temple, and the daily sacrifices are restored. The Antichrist agrees with the Jews to the conditions of the seven-year contract and restores the daily sacrifices, which will look pretty good on his part. It's interesting how once again, the devil imitates God by using a covenant agreement. We see this in the covenant that God made with Abraham:

As for me, this is my covenant with you: You will be the father of many nations. No longer will you be called Abram; your name will be called Abraham, for I have made you a father of many nations. I will make you very fruitful; I will make nations of you, and kings will come from you. I will establish my covenant as an everlasting covenant between me and you and your descendants after you for the generations to come, to be your God and the God of your descendants after you. The whole land of Canaan where you now reside as a foreigner, I will give as an everlasting possession to you and your descendants after you; and I will be their God.

Genesis 17:4-8 (NIV)

Just as God made a covenant with Abraham, the devil's plan is to also make a counterfeit covenant with Jewish people.

However, something unusual begins to happen after the seven-year covenant is made. The Antichrist begins to display his evil intent. The Antichrist, through cunning deceit, will win a majority of the world over to his favor, he will issue a mandate that everyone on the face of the earth is to make a mark on their right hand or forehead in order for them to buy or sell. He will give the false prophet the authority to follow through with his mandates, and eventually proclaim that he is the Savior of the world, and demand for all people to worship him. For those who oppose him and refuse to worship him will be persecuted.

At this point, the Jews are exempt from the command to worship the image because of the seven-year covenant agreement. However, somewhere in the midst of this seven-year covenant, the Antichrist will suddenly take away their daily sacrifices and replace them with the abomination of desolation.

The abomination of desolation is a sign of the end of the age in which Jesus spoke of in Matthew 24:15 (NIV), "So when you see standing in the holy place 'the abomination that causes desolation,' spoken of through the prophet Daniel—let the reader understand—"

What exactly is the abomination of desolation? The Hebrew root word for abomination is shaqats, which means "to be filthy," "to loath," "to abhor" (abomination of desolation: International Standard Bible Encyclopedia). The word abomination is often used to describe idolatrous worship practices. Once the Antichrist takes away the daily sacrifices to Yahweh, he will replace them with detestable pagan sacrifices in the Jewish Temple. It will be a blasphemous defilement of the Jewish Temple and an abomination to our living God.

When Jewish people, whom God adores, begin to realize they have made a terrible mistake, they will break the seven-year covenant with the Antichrist. They will repent before God and acknowledge that Jesus is the true Messiah. The eyes of the Jews will be opened to see their error, and all of Israel will be saved. The Jews came

out of the twelve tribes of Israel, and the apostle Paul
said,

> For I do not desire, brethren, that you should
> be ignorant of this mystery, lest you should be
> wise in your own opinion, that blindness in
> part has happened to Israel until the fullness
> of the Gentiles has come in. And so all Israel
> will be saved as it is written: "The Deliverer
> will come out of Zion."
>
> Romans 11:25-26 (NKJV)

It will be a wonderful time of rejoicing for the precious Jewish people! They will know and experience
the beautiful truth of God's grace through the only Savior of the world, the Lord Jesus Christ. The Antichrist
will then rage in his fury against the Jews because they
break the covenant, and his wrath will be directly targeted at them. When Jesus talked about the abomination of desolation, He said,

> "Therefore when you see the 'abomination
> of the desolation,' spoken of by Daniel the
> prophet, standing in the holy place" (whoever
> reads, let him understand), "then let those
> who are in Judea flee to the mountains. Let

him who is on the housetop not go down to
take anything out of his house."

Matthew 24:15-16 (NKJV)

It seems as though Jesus was urgent in His plea to
the beautiful Jewish people. At this point, the Antichrist is getting ready to spew his retribution on Jewish
people.

Jesus went on to tell them to pray that their flight
will not be in the winter. It will be a time of persecution
for Jewish people but also a glorious time of salvation
for them. The prophet Joel spoke of these days in Joel
2:32 (NIV), "And everyone who calls on the name of the
Lord will be saved; for on Mount Zion and in Jerusalem there will be deliverance, as the Lord has said, even
among the survivors whom the Lord calls."

God absolutely loves and adores the Jewish people.
He holds Israel very close to His heart, and He will bless
those who bless Israel. In Jeremiah 31:3 (NIV), it says,
"The Lord appeared to us in the past, saying: 'I have
loved you with an everlasting love; I have drawn you
with unfailing kindness. I will build you up again, and
you Virgin Israel, will be rebuilt.'" In verse 10, it says,

Hear the word of the Lord, you nations; proclaim it in distant coastlands: "He who scattered Israel will gather them and will watch

over his flock like a shepherd." For the Lord will deliver Jacob and redeem them from the hand of those stronger than they. They will come and shout for joy on the heights of Zion; they will rejoice in the bounty of the Lord—the grain, the new wine and olive oil, the young of the flock and herds. They will be like a well-watered garden, and they will sorrow no more.

Jeremiah 31:3 (NIV)

Never again will Jewish people weep with sorrow. God promises to deliver and redeem them, and they will shout for joy. Their tears will vanish forever, and they will dwell in the presence of Jesus. In Luke 6:21 (NIV), it says, "Blessed are you who weep now, for you will laugh." It is important to pray for Jerusalem. Just as Queen Esther prayed for the lives of the entire Jewish people who lived in Persia, we are to stand in prayer for them now. Mordecai told Esther that she shouldn't think that she would be spared if she neglected to plead for the Jews.

When Esther's words were reported to Mordecai, he sent back this answer: "Do not think that because you are in the king's house you alone of all the Jews will escape. For if you remain silent at this time, relief and deliverance for the Jews will arise from another place, but you and your father's family will perish. And who knows but that you have come to your royal position for such a time as this?"

Esther 4:12-14 (NIV)

We are in this together with Jewish people, and our prayers will be honored by God.

CHAPTER 10

The Rapture of the Church

There have been multitudes of questions in the minds of believers about the timing of the Rapture of the church. Over the years, there have been well-meaning scholars who are convinced that the church will not be here when the tribulation begins.

I cannot find a place in the Bible that declares the exact time and day the Lord will come to get his bride, commonly referred to as the Rapture of the church. Neither do we know when the sixth world empire will appear on the scene. The time of the Rapture is for only the Father to know; however, we are to look for the signs of the times.

The apostle Paul made a key statement about the timing of Christ's return.

Now, brethren, concerning the coming of our Lord Jesus Christ and our gathering together to him, we ask you, not to be soon shaken in mind or troubled, either by spirit or by word or by letter, as if from us, as though the day of Christ had come. Let no one deceive you by any means; for that Day will not come unless the falling away comes first, and the man of sin is revealed, the son of perdition, who opposes and exalts himself above all that is called God or that is worshipped, so that he sits as God in the temple of God, showing himself that he is God.

2 Thessalonian 2:1-4 (NKJV)

In this passage, the apostle Paul was keenly focused on the coming of Jesus and the Rapture taking place. He comforted the Christ-followers by encouraging them not to be troubled and told them that day will not come until a couple of things happen. I think it is important to remember that Paul said to not let our hearts be troubled. The first thing will be a falling away of believers, and the second thing will be the revealing of the man of sin. Paul did not want these followers of Christ to be fearful or be confused about the order of these events! According to this passage, the apostle Paul indicated there will not be the Rapture of the church until the man of sin is revealed.

I have pretty well established that we are living in world empire number five and that it is recognized in heaven by God Almighty. All signs are pointing to the establishment of world empire number six in the future. Jesus warned us about the great tribulation and that it is to come before the Rapture of the church. Notice that Jesus refers to the tribulation as the "great tribulation."

> For then there will be great tribulation, such as has not been since the beginning of the world until this time, no, nor ever shall be. And unless those days were shortened, no flesh would be saved; but for the elect's sake those days will be shortened.
>
> Matthew 24:21-22 (NKJV)

Jesus was clear that of all the tribulations that mankind has ever suffered, since the beginning of time, there is absolutely nothing that compares with the great tribulation of Christians. The intentions of the Antichrist are to rage war against God's people and to break their will. He succeeds in persecuting those people who do not take the mark of the beast on their forehead or right hand. His violent heavy hand of persecution upon God's people continues until Christ in His mercy appears and catches away the church. Jesus said that he would shorten those days of the great tribulation for the elect's sake. Even though no one knows the hour or the day of Jesus' return, I believe there are enough signs and markers in the Bible to point us to that glorious event. According to Matthew 24, Christ will return for his bride sometime during the great tribulation. There is a strong indication that the Rapture will bring the great tribulation to a screeching halt.

I believe Paul answered a very important question in 2 Thessalonians about the timing of the Rapture. A question that many Christians are asking today, "Which comes first, the Rapture or the tribulation?" If the Rapture comes first, then obviously, the believers in the Lord Jesus Christ will not go through the great tribulation. However, if the man of sin is revealed first, then the believers will go through the great tribulation. I don't think there is one person who would choose to go through the great tribulation. It would be much more pleasant to believe the church will skip the great tribulation, but in my perception, that is not what the Bible teaches. Please go with me as we dive into scripture that supports the idea of the Rapture occurring after the revealing of the man of sin. Please hear this, my friends, the wrath of God is not to be confused with the great tribulation! The wrath of God is reserved for those who take the mark of the beast and worship the beast. It is important to separate the wrath of God from the wrath of the Antichrist in order to have a clear understanding of the end times.

My hope is that the following scriptures and explanation will provide a clear understanding of the Rapture of the church. The apostle Paul makes this statement in regards to the Rapture of the church:

And now you know what is holding him back, so that he may be revealed at the proper time. For the secret power of lawlessness is already at work; but the one who now holds it back will continue to do so till he is taken out of the way. And then the lawless one will be revealed, whom the Lord Jesus will overthrow with the breath of his mouth and destroy by the splendor of his coming. The coming of the lawless one will be in accordance with how Satan works. He will use all sorts of displays of power through signs and wonders that serve the lie, and all the ways that wickedness deceives those who are perishing. They perish because they refused to love the truth and so be saved. For this reason God sends them a powerful delusion so that they will believe the lie and so that all will be condemned who have not believed the truth but have delighted in wickedness.

2 Thessalonian 2:6-12 (NIV)

Let's take a look at exactly what Paul was talking about when he said what is holding him back may be revealed at the proper time. In King James, this passage says: "What is restraining that he may be revealed in his own time." The Greek word "restrain" means "to hinder" or "to restrict." He who now restrains or "hinders" will do so until He is taken out of the way, and then the lawless one will be revealed. There is a popular belief within the Christian community that the word restrain, in this particular passage, is referring to the church or the Holy Spirit. Many writers and commentators have speculated that the apostle Paul was referring to the restrainer or hinderer as the one who is holding back the revealing of the lawlessness one. Many books have been written on this subject, and the strong view is that when the church is taken away, the man of sin will be revealed. Paul used the term "he" when he referred to the hinderer, which distinctly speaks of the male gender. The church has always been regarded as the bride, which would be the female gender.

The apostle Paul could have used the terms "bride," "elect," "church," or "the Holy Spirit" when referring to who must be taken away before the son of perdition is revealed. If he had used any of those terms, it would have resolved the controversy. There would not be any doubt in anyone's mind that the church would need to be raptured before the great tribulation takes place. I believe that Paul would have used terms like "she," "the bride," or "the church" if he was referring to the bride of Christ being taken out of the way. This teaching suggests the great tribulation will begin immediately following the church being taken away in the Rapture. I cannot find any scripture or passage anywhere in the Bible that supports that teaching.

When Paul used the term restrainer, it certainly would not be the beautiful bride of Christ that Paul was talking about. On the contrary, Paul was talking about something or someone that withholds, restricts, or hinders, and if it is not the Holy Spirit, then who is it that hinders?

When we examine the entire context of 2 Thessalonians 2:1-5, we can see that the disciples were asking about the coming of Christ. In verse five, Paul was reminding them that he had already shared the answer to their questions previously. As I stated before, Paul was encouraging them once again to not be troubled because Christ would not come until several events take place. The first event would be falling away, the second would be the revealing of the man of sin. There is not a doubt in my mind that Paul was referring to the devil as being the one who restrains. From the beginning of creation, in the Garden of Eden, the devil has tried everything to hinder the beautiful plan of God. It was the devil and the principalities of the air that attempted to restrain Daniel's prayer from being answered for twenty-one days, even though God had answered it on the first day. The devil is the accuser of the brethren, the father of lies, and the hinderer of God's people. We will take a look at why the restrainer will be taken away before the man of sin can be revealed.

There will be a defining moment in the future when the devil steps out of the way and surrenders his power and his seat of authority to the son of perdition! The devil will no longer restrain the Antichrist from making his appearance on earth. All of Satan's power will be transferred to the Antichrist at that moment in time. In Revelation 13:1 (NIV), John saw the dragon on the seashore, and in verse 2, we see the dragon giving all his power and authority over the Antichrist: "The dragon gave the beast his power and authority." In verse 4, it says, "People worshiped the dragon because he had given authority to the beast, and they also worshiped the beast and asked, 'Who is like the beast'? 'Who can wage war against it'?'" Here we see the dragon that was standing on the shore of the sea was the devil, and the beast that came up out of the sea is the Antichrist. At this point, the devil will transfer his authority over to the beast, which is the Antichrist.

When Paul mentioned the restrainer being taken out of the way, he was referring to the devil turning all of his power over to the Antichrist. It is a transfer of power from the devil to this one-world government leader. At that point in time, the devil will not be able to reclaim his power or his seat of authority since he has given it to his son, the Antichrist. The Antichrist will not be able to do or say anything on his own until the devil renders himself powerless. The devil will not surrender his power to anyone on earth except his own offspring. The man of sin will be able to do things that his father, the devil, could not do because the devil is a spirit, and he cannot be seen with the natural eye. The Antichrist will have a body, which can be seen with the natural eye. He will get much more accomplished in the way of destruction than the devil himself, and that is why the devil turns over his power of authority to him. There is only one thing that is hindering the Antichrist from appearing on the world scene, and that is the transfer of the devil's power and authority. The one that is restraining the Antichrist from being revealed is the devil, not the Holy Spirit!

As I stated before, there are multitudes of sermons, books, and articles that are robust in attempting to convince the Christian community that we will not be here when the great tribulation begins. Of course, that would be the most comforting thought that we could have.

However, it is important to keep our hearts open and our eyes watchful. For those who cling to the idea of the church not going through the great tribulation, there could be a great confusion of pandemic proportion when the persecution begins. I believe that is the reason that our loving God left us with all the signs and details about His coming in order for us to not be caught off guard.

My father occasionally would say that at some point in time in history, the world will wake up, and the man of sin will be sitting on their doorstep! There will be a moment in time when pandemonium will set in all over the Christian world, as well as the rest of the world. We are not the only people that are curious about the end times. In Matthew 24:3 (NIV), the disciples ask Jesus about the signs of his coming: "As Jesus was sitting on the Mount of Olives, the disciples came to Him privately. 'Tell us,' they said, 'When will this happen, and what will be the sign of your coming and of the end of the age?'"

Let's take a look at how Jesus answered the disciples' question:

> Jesus answered: "Watch out that no one deceives you. For many will come in my name, claiming, 'I am the Messiah,' and will deceive many. You will hear of wars and rumors of wars but see to it that you are not alarmed. Such things must happen, but the end is still

to come. Nation will rise against nation, and kingdom against kingdom. There will be famines and earthquakes in various places. All these are the beginning of birth pains. Then you will be handed over to be persecuted and put to death, and you will be hated by all nations because of me. At that time many will turn away from the faith and will betray and hate each other, and many false prophets will appear and deceive many people. Because of the increase of wickedness, the love of most will grow cold, but the one who stands firm to the end will be saved. And this gospel of the kingdom will be preached in the whole world as a testimony to all nations, and then the end will come."

Matthew 24:4-14 (NIV)

Jesus is letting the disciples know that in the end times, many will turn away from the faith, betray, hate each other, be deceived, and their love will grow cold. We can certainly see how love has grown colder in the days that we are living in. Anger, rage, and violence are on the rise in families, the workplace, in politics, and between nations. When Jesus was talking about the end times, He mentioned the gospel being preached in all the world. With the help of satellites, technology, missionaries, and other resources, we can see how the gospel will eventually be spread over the globe. Out of God's love and compassion, He will shorten the days of the great tribulation, and when He does, Jesus will burst through the clouds of glory to get His bride! The devil will no longer be able to persecute or accuse the saints of God.

As I mentioned earlier, in Daniel 9:27, it tells of a covenant made for one seven and of one who will cut off the daily sacrifices in the middle of the seven. Each week in prophecy represents a year which means a seven-year period. The great tribulation is set for a seven-year run, but Jesus cuts it short by His glorious coming.

> Then one of the elders answered, saying to me, "Who are these arrayed in white robes, and where did they come from?" And I said to him, "Sir, you know." So he said to me, "These are the ones who came out of the great tribulation, and washed their robes and made them white in the blood of the lamb."
>
> Revelation 7:13-14 (NKJV)

I do not have the answer to why God would allow the saints of God to experience something as horrifying as the great tribulation. But what I do know is that God is a God of love, justice, mercy, truth, and compassion.

God will not do anything that is not justified, and when He says there will be great tribulation, then it is justified in the eyes of God. Keep in mind, the great tribulation is orchestrated by the Antichrist, not God. When we look back at the Garden of Eden, we see the deception that occurred in the Garden of Eden was not orchestrated by God, it was the devil that deceived Adam and Eve. God created men and women with the power to make choices; otherwise, He would have an earth full of puppets that would be forced to worship God. God did not want His beautiful creation to worship Him out of control or compulsion. God chose to create mankind with the freedom of choice to worship Him from their heart of love for Him. His creation has always had the freedom to choose between good and evil. There will be nothing good about the great tribulation because this evil is orchestrated by the Antichrist.

We could ask this question, "Why did God allow His Son to suffer and die an agonizing death on an old rugged cross for the seed of Adam?" If only there could have been another way that we could have been redeemed and inherited eternal life. The answer is that it was the plan that suited God, and it was the righteousness of God that Jesus took all of the wraths that we deserved upon Himself so that we could go free! God ransomed us out of sin by the death and resurrection of His Son, Jesus Christ.

What hope, what truth that we will not only see Him face to face someday, but we will also live in peace, without hatred, pride, gossip, rejection, and greed! Just the thought of it makes me excited as a believer in Christ. That, my friend, is His plan of redemption for you and for me! He does not desire that even one person would perish.

As I reflect back to twenty-five years ago, when my granddaughter asked if God was crying, I recall thinking to myself, *That would be a great title for a book.* When I was pondering a title for this book, my mind went back to a particular day when my son (the father of this same granddaughter) stopped by our house with a gift for me. When I opened up the large gift box, I was left speechless when I looked upon a beautiful porcelain doll. The doll was holding a broken teddy bear in her hands and had real-life tears coming down her face. I instantly heard the Holy Spirit whisper, this is to confirm the title of the book, "Is God Crying?"

I couldn't stop gazing at the sad expression on the doll's face and the pouty lip that you would see on someone that is crying deeply. I thanked the Lord for confirming the title of the book and propped the doll up on our guest bed. She was my prize!

A few nights later, my husband decided not to disturb my sleep and proceeded to slip into the guest room to lie down. Later in the day, I went to straighten the guest bed, only to find my doll face down with her arm broken off. My sweet husband had no clue the doll was there and accidentally lay down on it. I fell to my knees sobbing as I recalled the tenderness in my son when he gave it to me and also how God had used that doll to speak to me. In my grief, I was crying out these words, "God, she is broken, and I am so sad." As I was convulsively crying and lamenting over this beautiful broken doll, I heard God softly whisper these words: "I am crying more than you think." As I picked the doll up, I suddenly realized her beautiful head was also broken. I held the doll close to me, and then through my sobs, I cried out again, "God, she is too broken, and now I can't fix her." I then heard the Lord say these words to me: "The world is more broken than you know."

If we could look at this broken world through God's eyes, we would cry too. The world is more broken than we could ever imagine. For many people, it is hard to imagine that we have a Father who cries over our pain. I have spent years mentoring women of all ages who have deep wounds. If a parent has a difficult time crying with their children when they are hurt, there is a good chance they themselves did not have a parent who had the ability to cry with them. Our heavenly Father is not like that! God cries over our hurts more than we think! Psalm 27:10 (NKJV), "When my father and mother forsake me, Then the Lord will take care of me."

We can find ourselves wondering if God knows how broken this world is. God knows our world is broken, and He cares more than we can know. In Isaiah 43:4-5 (NIV), it says, "Since you are precious and honored in my sight, and because I love you, I will give people in exchange for you, nations in exchange for your life. Do not be afraid, for I am with you." God loves the world so much that he not only would give a nation for us, but He also gave his Son for a ransom for our sins. That's how precious we are to Him and how much He loves and honors us.

God did not create a broken world. In the beginning, God created a world that was absolutely perfect! When the devil showed up in the Garden of Eden, he began to lure God's creation, and unfortunately, Adam and Eve fell for it. At that point, the devil began to engineer a plan for his kingdom here on earth. However, God engineered a better plan, which was His Son Jesus, to be our way out of the devil's kingdom. In 1 Peter 1:9 (NIV), it says, "But you are a chosen people, a royal priesthood, a holy nation, God's special possession, that you may declare the praises of him who called you out of darkness into his glorious light." When we accept God's plan, we are no longer of this earth's kingdom, but the kingdom of God dwells within us. There are a new heaven and new earth that awaits every Christ-follower! When that glorious Rapture takes place, and Jesus comes back to gather his children to Himself, we will dance, sing, and worship before the One who sits upon the throne.

CHAPTER 11

What Will the Rapture Be Like?

For most of my life, I have heard stories, listened to sermons, and have read books about how the events surrounding the Rapture happen. I have heard stories such as, there will be people driving in cars who will go off course and crash because the driver was raptured. Others say that airplanes and trains will crash because the conductor or pilot was raptured, and the passengers were not. I personally see it a different way as I ponder my thoughts about the Rapture of the church. Because of the great tribulation, there may not be enough Christians left here to say grace at the breakfast table. By the time the Rapture occurs, most of the church will be in the grave. That is why Jesus said that if He did not shorten the days of the tribulation, there would not even be one flesh saved. In Matthew 24:22 (NIV), Jesus said, "If those days had not been cut short, no one would survive, but for the sake of the elect those days will be shortened."

Paul wrote about the manner of how the coming of the Lord would take place in 1 Thessalonians 5:1-2 (NKJV), "But concerning the times and the seasons, brethren, you have no need that I should write to you. For you yourselves know perfectly that the day of the Lord so comes as a thief in the night." In my perception, Paul was saying the Rapture will not be a secret to the church because Paul stated that believers in Christ would know perfectly about his coming. However, the Rapture of the church may not be an event the world will necessarily be aware of. The only people that may have that privy information are the people that are involved in it, the Christians. Consequently, there will not be a publicized Rapture of the church where the world will know what's going on. The Christians will be the only people that hear the trumpet sound, and the dead will come out of those tombs to meet the Lord in the air, without a casket or empty grave disturbed. The believers in Jesus Christ that are left, will be caught up to meet them in the air. The apostle Paul clearly describes the Rapture:

> For the Lord Himself will descend from heaven with a shout, with the voice of an archangel, and with the trumpet of God. And the

dead in Christ will rise first. Then we who are alive and remain shall be caught up together with them in the clouds to meet the Lord in the air. And thus we shall always be with the Lord. Therefore comfort one another with these words.

1 Thessalonians 4:16-18 (NKJV)

And it will all happen in a quick twinkling of the eye. Keep in mind that believers will have invisible, immortal bodies that can walk through walls, like Jesus. The reason I say this is because if the Rapture was advertised, the man of sin would lose credibility with the rest of the world who has the mark of the beast in their foreheads or their right hand. Please keep in mind that this Antichrist has been convincing multitudes that Christ did not raise from the dead and there was no resurrection.

The world will not miss a beat because there will absolutely be no sign of anyone being caught up in the air. There will not even be a blade of grass or a grain of sand disturbed on any grave anywhere! When I think about a thief breaking into a home, he normally would be as quiet as a mouse. Most people would not even be aware of his presence because the thief is intentional about being silent. The thief can come and go quickly, without us even noticing he has been there, until afterward. Paul uses the analogy of a thief because the coming of Christ for His bride will be that way, quickly and quietly. Not every eye will see this event, but every eye will see Christ at the battle of Armageddon. Jesus said in Matthew 24:24 that even the elect may be deceived. It is extremely important for the elect to understand how the Rapture takes place so that we do not fall away, take the mark of the beast, or be deceived.

Jesus said in Matthew 24:29 that immediately after the tribulation of those days, the sun will be darkened, and the moon will not give its light; the stars will fall from heaven, and the powers of the heavens will be shaken. Yes, my friends, the great tribulation will come to an end, it will come to an end! When Jesus shortens the great tribulation with His coming, the only people left on the face of the earth are those who have taken the mark of the beast. All of God's people are gone in the twinkle of an eye and the last trump. Immediately following the Rapture, the wrath of God begins to be poured out on those with the mark of the beast! The wrath of God begins with plagues, water turned to blood, scorching heat, body sores, the world inhabitants plunged into darkness. The wrath of God is reserved for after the Rapture takes place and will be poured out on those who have taken the mark of the beast and worship the Antichrist.

I have listened to many preachers, teachers, and theologians teach that there will be those who are left here on earth after the Rapture, and they will have another chance to accept Jesus as their Savior. If that would be the case, those who accept the Lord after the Rapture would experience the wrath of God following the Rapture. The children of God will not experience the wrath of God. It would also mean that we would need another Rapture, and I cannot find a passage in the Bible that supports the theory that there will be multiple Raptures!

During the time of the great tribulation, there will be every opportunity for every person to turn to Christ and for every sinner to be saved. There will be a time of revival that perhaps we have never experienced before. In Revelation 5:8-10 (NIV), John saw the Lamb take the scroll, and they sang a new song.

> And they sang a new song, saying: "You are worthy to take the scroll and to open its seals, because you were slain and with your blood you purchased for God persons from every tribe and language and people and nation. You have made them to be a kingdom and priests to serve our God, and they will reign on the earth."
>
> Revelation 5: 9-10 (NIV)

This passage tells us that God invites every person from every tribe, language, and people to accept Jesus as their Savior. Whether we live in the Free World, Communist World, or the Third World, that invitation is for all people. Jesus shed His blood for all people to be saved, and God will be merciful right down to the last minute. This gives us reason to be in fervent prayer for revival during these days of tribulation and persecution. I believe many people will turn to Christ during this time of great persecution. However, there will be that moment in time when God dispatches His Son to break through the portals of heaven, at the sound of a trumpet, to gather the dead in Christ first, and those that are still alive will be caught up to meet the Lord in the air and so forever be with the Lord!) The apostle Paul made this statement about the natural body and concerning the immortal body:

> Now this I say, brethren, that flesh and blood cannot inherit the kingdom of God; nor does corruption inherit incorruption. Behold, I tell you a mystery: We shall not all sleep, but we shall all be changed—in a moment, in the twinkling of an eye, at the last trumpet. For the trumpet will sound, and the dead will be raised incorruptible, and we shall be changed.
> 1 Corinthians 15:50-52 (NKJV)

Paul talks about two-time elements in this passage, one is a moment and the other—a twinkling of an eye. Paul could have just said in a moment, or he could have said in the twinkle of an eye. Paul could have even stretched the time element into an hour, a week, or even a year. Paul was speaking under the inspiration of the Holy Spirit, and what he had to say was coming right from the power of God! When we think of a twinkle of an eye, we understand the twinkle of a man's eye, the twinkle from the eye of a horse, or any living creature that has a lid over the eye. This lid moves up and down to cleanse the eyeball, and its movement is quicker than we can snap our fingers. That is how instantly quick the Rapture of the church will be.

However, if we believe there is going to be another Rapture after the first Rapture, then the twinkle of an eye is stretched into however many years a person could think up. If we embrace the theory that Christ will rapture His church more than one time, then we might as well believe there could be multiple Raptures. If I could find scriptures or passages in the Bible to support that belief, I would certainly want to believe it. What counts is what God's Word says about this subject, no matter how much anyone, including myself, wants to believe.

My friends, we cannot afford to think that we will escape the great tribulation or that somehow we will get another chance after the Rapture occurs. If my father was right about the time element of the great tribulation, it could mean that many people may be deceived if they believe that Jesus will take us all out of here before the great tribulation. The devil himself has been trying to deceive God's people since the Garden of Eden when he convinced Adam and Eve that they would not die if they ate the fruit. In God's great love for us, He has made us aware of what we should look for as we approach the end times.

If I personally did not have any knowledge of the end times, but I simply used common sense about the subject, I would tend to think it would not make sense for the Antichrist to persecute the people left here on earth following the Rapture of the church. If the church has already been raptured, there would not be anyone here on earth for the Antichrist to persecute. On the contrary, the persecution of Christians brought on by the Antichrist is targeted to the believers.

I have heard arguments that attempt to reason that the church will be raptured and not go through the great tribulation because the Bible says that God did not appoint us to wrath. Some have made the following verse part of their doctrine as far as the convincing factor that we will not go through the great tribulation.

In 1 Thessalonian 5:9 (NKJV), it says, "For God did not appoint us to wrath, but to obtain salvation through our Lord Jesus Christ." If the great tribulation was considered the same as the wrath of God, then I would agree with that theory. However, if we could recognize the great tribulation as a completely different event than the wrath of God, our eyes would be open to the truth.

Jesus tells us that after the tribulation of those days, the wrath of God will begin for those who have rejected and cursed God.

> Immediately after the tribulation of those days the sun will be darkened, and the moon will not give its light; the stars will fall from heaven, and the powers of the heavens will be shaken. Then the sign of the Son of Man will appear in heaven, and then all the tribes of the earth will mourn, and they will see the Son of Man coming on the clouds of heaven with power and great glory.
>
> Matthew 24:29-30 (NKJV)

This passage suggests the order of things to happen following the great tribulation. In my perception, the wrath of God will be poured out, followed by the Battle of Armageddon, where all the earth will mourn when they see Jesus and His saints coming in power on of clouds of heaven. In Revelation 1:7 (NIV), "Look, he is coming with the clouds," and "every eye will see him, even those who pierced him"; and all peoples on earth "will mourn because of him." So shall it be! Amen.

In Revelation 16:1-21 (NIV), John talks about the wrath of God being poured out on those who have the mark of the beast and who worship the beast.

> Then I heard a loud voice from the temple saying to the seven angels, "Go, pour out the seven bowls of God's wrath on the earth." The first angel went and poured out his bowl on the land, and ugly, festering sores broke out on the people who had the mark of the beast and worshipped its image.
>
> Revelation 16:1-2 (NIV)

There will not be any Christians on earth during that time of God's wrath because they have been raptured. The wrath of God will continue until the battle of Armageddon.

I want to mention another part of this revelation that God gave to John.

> Then war broke out in heaven. Michael and his angels fought against the dragon, and the dragon and his angels fought back. But he was not strong enough, and they lost their place in heaven. The great dragon was hurled

down—that ancient serpent called the devil,
or Satan, who leads the whole earth astray.
He was hurled to the earth, and his angels
with him.

Revelation 12:7-9 (NIV)

In verse 12, it says, "Therefore rejoice, you heavens
and you who dwell in them! But woe to the earth and
the sea, because the devil has gone down to you! He is
filled with fury because he knows that his time is short."

I do not know if that war in heaven has already taken
place or when it will take place, but I do know that when
it does, there will be wickedness like we have never seen
on the earth before. Woe to the inhabitants of the earth,
whenever sin is out of control and the devil has come
with great wrath. The devil and all his demonic forces
will be at full throttle around the globe. God must cry
when He looks sadly at the rapid degeneration in the
morals of the world over the past years. Moral decay has
crept into schools, families, government, churches, social media, movies, and places of employment. It seems
like the world system has become Babylon, talked
about in the seventeenth chapter of Revelation. Satan
has been seeking whom he may devour and deceiving
people by the multitudes. When the devil and his angels realize they no longer have access to heavens or to
go up to the throne to accuse the brethren and that he

has truly been kicked out of heaven, he knows his time is short!

The apostle Paul wrote to young Timothy these words:

> But know this, that in the last days perilous times will come: for men will be lovers of themselves, lovers of money, boasters, proud, blasphemers, disobedient to parents, un-thankful, unholy, unloving, unforgiving, slanderers, without self-control, brutal, despisers of good, traitors, headstrong, haughty, lovers of pleasure rather than lovers of God, having a form of godliness but denying its power. And from such people turn away!
>
> 2 Timothy 3:1-5 (NKJV)

I am persuaded to believe that this great escalation of sin, lawlessness, rebellion, and wickedness is possibly the result of the devil being cast out of heaven. It has been moving at such a rapid pace we could say it's almost out of hand. The Bible originally was written in scrolls and not divided into chapters. When it was in scroll form, it went straight from the devil being cast out of heaven into when John saw the beast coming up out of the sea.

If we wanted to put the end times in some kind of order, it may look something like this:

1. The birth of Jesus, our Messiah.
2. The devil being cast out of heaven and making war on Christ's offspring.
3. The Antichrist and the false prophet rising up on the earth.
4. The Great Tribulation where the saints are persecuted and killed.
5. The Rapture of the church.
6. The wrath of God poured out on those who took the mark of the beast.
7. Christ coming with His saints for the battle of Armageddon.
8. The Antichrist and the false prophet thrown alive into eternal fire.
9. The devil is bound, thrown into the bottomless pit for one thousand years.
10. One thousand years of peace with Jesus ruling the earth.
11. The devil is loosed out of hell for a short time after the one thousand years.
12. The devil and his army surround Israel to wage war.
13. Fire comes down from heaven and devours the devil and his army.

14. The devil is cast into fire and brimstone, where the Antichrist and the false prophet are.
15. The great white throne of judgment where the books are opened. A new heaven and new earth.

Conclusion

As I come to my closing thoughts about the events surrounding the end times, I thought this passage would be appropriate:

Then I, Daniel, looked, and there before me stood two others, one on this bank of the river and one on the opposite bank. One of them said to the man clothed in linen, who was above the waters of the river, "How long will it be before these astonishing things are fulfilled?" The man clothed in linen, who was above the waters of the river, lifted his right hand and his left hand toward heaven, and I heard him swear by him who lives forever, saying, "It will for a time, times and half a time. When the power of the holy people has been finally broken, all things will be completed." I heard, but I did not understand. So I asked, "My Lord, what will the outcome of all this be?" He replied, "Go your way, Daniel, because the words are rolled up and sealed until the time of the end. Many will be purified, made spotless and refined, but the wicked will continue to be wicked. None of the wicked will understand, but those who are wise will understand. From the time that the daily sacrifice is abolished and the abomination that causes desolation is set up, there will be 1,290 days. Blessed is the one who waits for and reaches the end of the 1,335 days. As for you, go your way till the end. You will rest, and then at the end of the days you will rise to receive your allotted inheritance."

Daniel 12:5-13 (NIV)

God let Daniel know that when the power of the holy people has finally been broken, all things will be completed. I firmly believe the holy people that God was referring to are those suffering the great tribulation, and when they are broken, the end will come. We have walked from the prophetic book of Daniel to the prophetic book of Revelation. In the final chapter of the book of Daniel, the Lord told Daniel the words of the book were rolled up and sealed until the end of time.

Daniel questioned the Lord in verses 8-9 and said, "I heard, but I did understand. So I asked, 'My Lord, what will the outcome of all this be'? He replied, 'Go your way, Daniel, because the words are rolled up and sealed until the time of the end.'"

In Revelation 5:2 (NIV), the angel asked who was worthy to break the seal and open the scroll: "And I saw a mighty angel proclaiming in a loud voice, 'Who is worthy to break the seals and open the scroll'?" It goes on to say that only the lamb was worthy to break the seals and open the scrolls. It is interesting that in the book of Daniel, the Lord told Daniel to seal up the words of the book until the end. In the book of Revelation, the seals of the scroll are to be opened, and John was instructed to not seal up the words of this book.

The angel told John:

> Then he told me, "Do not seal up the words of the prophecy of this scroll, because the time is near. Let the one who does wrong continue to do wrong; let the vile person continue to be vile; let the one who does right continue to do right; and let the holy person continue to be holy."
>
> Revelation 22:10-11(NIV)

And then Jesus spoke to John in verses 12-13 and said, "Look, I am coming soon! My reward is with me, and I will give to each person according to what they have done. I am the Alpha and the Omega, the First and the Last, The Beginning and the End."

We cannot be positive when those scrolls are to be opened in the book of Revelation. It is interesting that Daniel was told the scrolls were sealed up and was told to go his way and wait for his reward, but John was instructed to keep the scrolls open because the time is near. This indicates to me that when the prophetic words in the Bible come to pass, there will be no need to keep the scrolls sealed because the end times have come. Since the book of Daniel and the book of Revelation tie into together, it makes sense that God's prophetic time clock will be fulfilled.

We do not want our minds to be tricked or deluded in any way. When we know the truth, it will set us free. I am so grateful that God has revealed the truth concerning the end times to anyone who seeks it. When God reveals His truth, it clears the air about where we came from, where we are at, and where we are going. On the other hand, when we live in doubt, we are double-minded, and we are not free. I personally do not know every detail about the events of the end times, but I am confident the Holy Spirit will reveal these things to us as we pursue His plan.

My friends, I encourage you to ask the Holy Spirit to open your awareness of what I have shared with you. I am not positive that my father or myself have hit the perfect target on the events concerning the end times, but I am positive as believers, we are not to be engulfed in fear. On the contrary, we are to be filled with hope as we look forward to the coming of the Lord Jesus Christ. The apostle Paul suffered overwhelming persecution and suffering for the sake of Christ. Paul put it in the right perspective when he said that to be absent from the body is to be present with Christ. Paul said in 2 Corinthians 5:8 (NKJV), "We are confident, yes, well pleased rather be absent from the body and be present with the Lord." This world is not our home, and it never has been. We have a home being prepared for us, and it is beautiful! I can recall my daddy saying: "This is not our home, we are pilgrims, just passing through."

Jesus said,

> Blessed are those who are persecuted because of righteousness, for theirs is the kingdom of heaven. Blessed are you when people insult you, persecute you and falsely say all kinds of evil against you because of me. Rejoice and be glad, because great is your reward in heaven, for in the same way they persecuted the prophets who were before you.
>
> Matthew 5:10-12 (NIV)

As believers, and according to these passages, we should not be surprised that we will be persecuted.

God is a God of love, mercy, and justice. He is not a harsh disciplinary father who is constantly checking to see if we have messed up. If you have not tasted the love of Father, who absolutely adores His creation, I encourage you to pause to ask Him to reveal Himself to you. You will find a heavenly Father who has been waiting for you, with His arms wide open to hold you, and He will hold you for as long as you want to stay. He weeps with you when you hurt, He rejoices with you when you celebrate, as any good dad would do. He has made a way for you to forgive those who have hurt you and for you to be forgiven by Him. If we confess our sins, He is able to forgive us our sins and cleanse us from all unrighteousness. In 1 John 1:9 (NIV), it says, "If we confess our sins, he is faithful and just and will forgive us our sins and purify us from all unrighteousness."

You may be reading this information, and at one time, you loved the Lord and obeyed Him, but you strayed from His love. Or, you may even think that you have strayed too far and done too much for His redeeming love to accept you. I encourage you to return to God and ask Him to help you fully understand His grace and His truth. We can never stray so far from God that He will not accept us back into His loving arms if we ask him. When Jesus went to the cross, He willingly took the wrath that we deserved upon Himself so that we could be free from all guilt and shame. He offers each one of us hope and eternal life and gives us an opportunity to spend eternity with Him in a beautiful place called heaven. All that God requires of us is that we confess to Him that we are sinners and that we need Jesus as our Savior. We can ask Him to come into our hearts, and He will reside there forever. It's as simple as that! He did not make it difficult for us to make Him our personal Savior.

It's not about doing something good for God or about being good for God. He has already done the work for us on the cross. He wants us to come to Him just as we are so that He can give us the free gift of salvation. We do not need to change or to get better so that He will accept us. He is the one who makes the change in us, and He makes our life better from the inside out! In John 6:37 (NKJV), Jesus said, "All that the Father gives Me will come to Me, the one who comes to Me I will by no means cast out." He will never turn anyone away from this gift of salvation. Jesus will never cast us away when we come to Him and ask Him into our heart.

I will push the pause button here for a moment and praise our living God for His unfailing love for His creation. I rejoice that God did not leave us in the dark concerning the end times and that He reveals the mysteries of the end times to His children. I am humbled that I have the opportunity to share my father's writings and my thoughts with those who care to listen.

As I approach my final thoughts, may you know that these writings are not intended to bring fear or judgment but to bring hope and rejoicing that we have a God who is preparing a better home for us to look forward to? I lay no claims on being a theologian, scholar, or professional expert on this subject matter. However, I sense a responsibility to share what I understand as being the end times with others. My heart is compassionate, tender, and concerned for the body of Christ and for those who may not know the love of our Savior Jesus Christ. I respect the fact that this message may not be fully embraced and perhaps rejected simply because it includes a huge amount of persecution and suffering for the Christians in the future.

I encourage you, dear friend, to ponder these things and study the Bible fervently. Draw close to the inner chambers of God's heart and let Him speak to you about these latter days. Whether we believe the church will be taken away in the Rapture before the great tribulation, or we believe the church will go through the great tribulation, or perhaps a part of it, we all need to be ready to meet Jesus.

As I write these final thoughts, I encourage you to fix your eyes upon these promises:

Now I saw a new heaven and a new earth, for the first heaven and the first earth had passed away. Also there was no more sea. Then I, John, saw the holy city, New Jerusalem, coming down out of heaven from God, prepared as a bride adorned for her husband. And I heard a loud voice from heaven saying, "Behold, the tabernacle of God is with men, and He will dwell with them, and they shall be His people. God Himself will be with them and be their God. And God will wipe away every tear from their eyes; there shall be no more death, nor sorrow, nor crying. There shall be no more pain, for the former things have passed away." Then He who sat on the throne said, "Behold, I make all things new." And He said to me, "Write, for these words are true and faithful." And He said to me, "It is done! I am the Alpha and Omega, the Beginning and the End. I will give of the fountain of the water of life freely to him who thirsts. He who overcomes shall inherit all things, and I will be his God and he shall be My son.

Revelation 21:1-7 (NKJV)

As Christians, we have a hope that is eternal and a home called heaven! The beauty of heaven is more than we could ever comprehend. A place where there is no more sorrow, no more rejection, no more persecution, no more abuse or tears. There will be no more crying, my dear friends! God will wipe away every tear, and instead of God crying with us, He will be singing and rejoicing with us! Praise our living, merciful God Almighty! He will give freely the water of life to those who thirst. For those who overcome, they will inherit the kingdom. Matthew 24:13 (ESV), "But the one who endures to the end shall be saved."

CPSIA information can be obtained
at www.ICGtesting.com
Printed in the USA
FSHW020038170621

9 781637 693469